The far left in the English Revolution 1640 to 1660

The far left in the English Revolution 1640 to 1660

Brian Manning

BOOKMARKS

London, Chicago and Sydney

The Far Left in the English Revolution 1640 to 1660 – Brian Manning
First published 1999
Bookmarks Publications Ltd, c/o 1 Bloomsbury Street, London WC1B 3QE, England
Bookmarks, PO Box 16085, Chicago, Illinois 60616, USA
Bookmarks, PO Box A338, Sydney South, NSW 2000, Australia
Copyright © Bookmarks Publications Ltd

ISBN 1 898876 47 9 (Hardback)
ISBN 1 898876 48 7 (Paperback)

Printed by Larkham Printing and Publishing
Cover by Sherborne Design

Contents

Brian Manning is emeritus Professor of History at the University of Ulster. His previous books include *The English People and the English Revolution* (Second Edition, London, 1991), *1649: The Crisis of the English Revolution* (London, 1992) and *Politics, Religion and the English Civil War*, of which he was editor and the contributor of the chapter on 'The Aristocracy and the Downfall of Charles I'.

Preface

All historical studies begin from the framing of questions to be addressed to the evidence left by the past: questions which in the process of research will be revised or abandoned, and will give rise to further and often unexpected questions. In the case of this book the questions arise from hypotheses formulated in Marxist historiography, because those are relevant to 'history from below' and focus on the 'poor', especially the wage workers, and those who claimed to speak for them.

At the time of the English Revolution it was common to make a tripartite division of society into the gentry, 'the middling sort' and 'the poor'. The first and second of those categories have occupied the attentions of historians—the first much more than the second—in assessing the causes and course of the revolution, but the third has been largely neglected. It is the intention of this book to make a preliminary attempt to remedy this omission.

The first chapter considers the economic setting and the growth of the wage earning class in the context of developing capitalism. The second chapter analyses the ideological setting, especially the important role of religion.

The Levellers provided much of the philosophy and programme of radicalism, to which the millenarian Fifth Monarchists and the Quakers added important elements. Such radicalism may be described as being on the 'left' of the revolution, being more radical than the Presbyterians, Independents and Republicans who dominated the revolution. But the focus of this book is upon those who stood further to the left than the leaderships of the Levellers, Fifth Monarchists and Quakers. The 'far left' in the English Revolution is defined in terms of ideas, which sought to promote a shift in the revolution towards establishing social and economic equality, and in terms of practice, which involved taking more militant action than the established leaders, in order to achieve some of the aims of the far left, but also of the left in general. The latter is the subject of chapter three.

1

Attention is concentrated on those who attempted to speak for the poor and the more deprived sections of society. Questions arise about how far they reflected attitudes and aspirations of the poor, who remain almost entirely silent in the sources. Questions also arise about cultural differences between dominant and subordinate classes, and about obstacles to revolutionary action by the poor.

The third chapter deals with two attempts at armed insurrection arising from the radical or left milieu of the 1650s, and at the same time puts the focus on two individual revolutionaries who emerged from the ranks of plebeians. The poor generally did not rise in revolt against the republican governments established by the revolution. But viewing the period from below brings with it analysis of the formation of classes, the appearance of class conflicts, and explanation of the course which the revolution eventually took. It is also the purpose of this book to consider aspects of Marxist historiography that relate to its themes, and to place the English Revolution in the history of struggles for social justice.

I have been enlightened by discussions with Paul Blackledge and Andy Wood, and Norah Carlin gave me valuable advice on the first draft of this book. Chapter one is a revised version of my contribution to *Essays on Historical Materialism*, edited by John Rees (Bookmarks, London, 1998), and a substantial part of chapter three appeared in *Socialist History* 1 (1993). This book was developed in a series of papers given at the annual conferences of *Marxism*, organised by the British and Irish Socialist Workers parties in London and Dublin, and I have profited from the discussions on those occasions.

Brian Manning, May 1999

Chapter 1

Labour

Marx and Engels held that exploitation of labour and conflict of classes were the fundamental factors in history from earliest times to the present. As they said in the *Communist Manifesto*: 'The history of all past society has consisted in the development of class antagonisms, antagonisms that assumed different forms at different epochs. But whatever form they may have taken, one fact is common to all past ages, viz: the exploitation of one part of society by the other... The whole history of mankind...has been a history of class struggles, contests between exploiting and exploited, ruling and oppressed classes': slave owners and slaves, feudal lords and peasants, employers and wage workers.[1] It is a fundamental idea of Marxism that the exploiters form the ruling classes, dominating directly or indirectly the state, the law, ideology and culture, and the exploited are the ruled classes. Exploitation determines the distribution of power, and power in turn enforces and defends exploitation. Not every conflict between groups in society springs from class antagonism, but when two groups stand in a relation of exploiters and exploited it is a class relation; and when one group seeks to exploit another group, and the latter group resists, they become engaged in class struggle.[2]

In volume one of *Capital* Marx defined exploitation in terms of 'necessary' and 'surplus' labour: necessary labour was that part of labour required for the subsistence of the producer, and surplus labour was that part of labour appropriated from the producer by the exploiter. The means of subsistence include food, clothing, housing and fuel, which vary according to the climate and from one historical period to another. The number and extent of 'necessary wants, as also the modes of satisfying them, are themselves the product of historical development, and depend

---

1   K Marx and F Engels, *Selected Works*, vol I (2 vols, Moscow, 1949-50), pp28, 33, 50.
2   K Kautsky, *The Materialist Conception of History*, J H Kautsky (ed), (New Haven, 1988), pp252, 254.

therefore to a great extent...on the habits and degree of comfort' in which the particular class of producers has been formed. 'Capital has not invented surplus labour': it existed in ancient Greece and Rome. It was appropriated by feudal barons and American slaveowners, as well as by modern landowners and capitalists. Marx illustrated it by drawing a parallel between the medieval peasant and the modern factory worker. 'Suppose', he said, 'the working day consists of six hours of necessary labour and six hours of surplus labour. Then the free labourer gives the capitalist every week 36 hours of surplus labour. It is the same as if he worked three days in the week for himself and three days in the week gratis for the capitalist.' The medieval serf owed labour services to his lord and worked, say, three days a week on his own plot of ground and three days a week on his lord's land. 'Three days surplus labour in the week,' concluded Marx, 'remain three days that yield no equivalent to the labourer himself', whether it is the labour services of the medieval peasant or the wage labour of the modern factory worker.

The point Marx is making is that both feudalism and capitalism exploit labour, but by different means as they are different modes of production. Under the feudal mode of production in general the producer was in possession of the means of production (land and tools) and under no economic compulsion to work for a lord or to pay rent. Therefore, in order to get the peasants to hand over part of their labour or product, the lords exercised non-economic coercion by jurisdictional and political means, backed by armed force, to extract this surplus. But at the core of the capitalist mode of production, the producers are not in possession of the means of production, and as a result cannot provide for their own subsistence or produce their own commodities for sale on the market. Having only their labour power, they must sell it to the capitalist for a wage in order to survive. They do not sell their labour itself, but their labour power—that is the capacity for labour—for if they sold their labour they would be selling themselves and so become slaves. The free worker takes 'his labour power to market and offers it for sale as a commodity "belonging" to him, a thing that he "possesses".' Thus a human function is transformed into a commodity and so dehumanised. As the number of peasants who had insufficient land for their subsistence under the feudal system increased, they were subjected to economic coercion to hire themselves out as wage labourers for part or all of their time in order to make ends meet, but the system still remained feudal.[3]

3   K Marx, *Capital*, vol I, ch VI (Moscow, 1954), pp226-227; vol III, ch XLVII (London, 1959); Introduction by Engels to Marx, 'Wage Labour and Capital', in K Marx and F Engels, op cit, pp66-73; G Lukács, *History and Class Consciousness*, translated by R Livingstone

The greater part of mankind, however, will not be prepared to sweat hard to produce the fruits of the earth for a minority to consume unless either coerced or enticed into doing so. This simple truth was recognised in all ages, and the dilemma faced by the privileged few was how to devise and operate means of ensuring that the poor did labour assiduously.

Broadly speaking, under feudalism and before the English Revolution the answer was to keep them poor so that they had to work hard to survive. But after the English Revolution, and under capitalism, the answer was increasingly but unevenly adopted that the poor would have an incentive to work longer and harder if by so doing they could acquire better food and clothing, as well as more household goods, which became more available at prices they could afford as a result of capitalist production in agriculture and industry.[4]

Maurice Dobb wrote that 'basically the mode of production under feudalism was the petty mode of production': production by peasants and artisans who possessed the means of production. Part of their product was extracted from them to support the feudal ruling class, and so 'the crucial class struggle under feudalism' was between the small producers and the feudal lords.[5] The struggle was over the distribution of the surplus, with the lords seeking to obtain more and the producers seeking to give less. With the disappearance of serfdom the battle took place over rents, fines (payments on entry into a tenancy) and heriots (payments on the death of a tenant). But there was not a state of continuous conflict between peasants and lords. Peasants commonly accepted tenancies on the terms offered without complaint, and lords generally recognised obligations 'to foster and protect the interests of their tenants, who accepted them naturally as social as well as tenurial superiors'. It was not usually in the interests of lords to provoke peasant resistance.[6]

A question that arises here is whether the peasants and artisans formed a single class—that is, a class of petty or small producers—or two distinct classes. 'The manipulation involved in buying the product

(London, 1971), pp91-92; R Brenner, 'The Agrarian Roots of European Capitalism', *Past and Present* 97 (1982), pp29-30, reprinted in T H Aston and C H E Philpin, *The Brenner Debate* (Cambridge, 1985).

4 J Hatcher, 'Labour, Leisure and Economic Thought Before the 19th Century', *Past and Present* 160 (1998), pp65, 67-71, 92-95, 96-97, 104-109.

5 M Dobb, 'From Feudalism to Capitalism', in R H Hilton (ed), *The Transition from Feudalism to Capitalism* (London, 1976), pp165-167; F Engels, *Socialism: Utopian and Scientific* (London, 1993), pp89, 110-111.

6 C E Searle, 'Custom, Class Conflict and Agrarian Capitalism', *Past and Present* 110 (1986), pp111, 113, 118-119; M Hicks, *Bastard Feudalism* (London, 1995), pp91-93.

cheap from the artisan and selling dear in the market was not strictly analogous to the exercise of non-economic coercion by the landowner to extract feudal rent from the peasant.' The artisan sold his product to the merchant, who appropriated the surplus by exchange in the form of part of the value of the product, but the landlord did not buy the product of the peasant. Instead he siphoned off his surplus in the form of rent and other dues. Nevertheless, production in the case of both peasants and artisans took place in small units based on the family and household: 'No doubt the similarities of small scale production produced similarities of outlook', and exploitation by landlord or merchant 'created similar antagonisms'. Although the methods of extracting the surplus were different, both took place within a mode of production dominated by large feudal landlords to whom the merchants were subordinate.[7]

This remained the situation during the transition from feudalism to capitalism, except that, in addition to exploitation by feudal lords, small producers were exploited by emerging capitalists. In a bourgeois revolution both the aristocracy and the bourgeoisie are exploiting classes and, as Boris Porchnev pointed out, concentration on those two classes may lead to missing or effacing the conflict between them and the exploited, which he called 'the really fundamental antagonism between classes'.[8] That lay at the heart of the English Revolution.

There were three forms of labour in society at the time of the English Revolution: (i) the producer possessed sufficient means of production for subsistence and labour took place within the family and household unit, partly for domestic consumption and partly for sale; (ii) the producer possessed insufficient means of production for subsistence and combined labour in the family and household unit, for domestic consumption and sale, with labour outside that unit for wages from an employer; (iii) the producer did not possess the means of production and obtained his subsistence wholly by labour for wages. There were legions of workers who were paid for a service which was for the personal consumption of their employer rather than for the production of wealth, such as domestic servants and jobbing artisans. But there were increasing numbers of workers, including other types of servants and artisans, and agricultural labourers, whose services were hired for the purposes of production rather than the consumption of wealth. These last were, in

---

7   R H Hilton, *Class Conflict and the Crisis of Feudalism* (revised second edition, London, 1990), pp7-8, 83-84, 108-109.
8   B Porchnev, 'Popular Uprisings in France Before the Fronde, 1623-1648', in P J Coveney (ed), *France in Crisis 1620-1657* (London, 1977), p91.

Marx's definition, truly the 'wage workers', and the employers who extracted the surplus labour from them were capitalists. Capitalism involved the exploitation of wage labour: wage labour created capital and capitalists and in doing so, by Marx's definition, formed the 'working class' or proletariat.[9] There are signs during the English Revolution that lines of conflict were being increasingly drawn between landed peasants and landless peasants and between employers and wage workers.

The crucial distinction was between small producers who possessed the means of production and had part of the product of their labour transferred to landlords and merchants, and wage labourers who did not possess the means of production and had only their labour power, which they exchanged for wages. There were wage labourers under feudalism as well as under capitalism, but the transition from feudalism to capitalism involved an increasing proportion of wage labour being exploited by capitalist employers rather than by feudal lords and feudal peasants. Small producers and wage labourers formed the labour force of pre-industrial society. Small producers as well as wage labourers earned their livings by long hours of hard manual labour, and the basic distinction of status in traditional society was between those lower strata who gained their livelihood by working with their hands and those upper strata who received their livelihood without having to engage in manual labour.[10] However, small producers were often also employers of labour and therefore were themselves exploiters, as well as being exploited by feudal lords and merchants.

Norah Carlin has raised the question of the position of wage workers in the English Revolution.[11] The purpose of this chapter is to consider the transition of some small producers into capitalists and others into proletarians, the subsuming of wage labourers into the capitalist mode of production, and the emerging class differences which shaped the course and outcome of the revolution.

The extent and limits of proletarianisation

Capitalism and a market economy were developing in 17th century England, involving increased production for the market by means of employing more wage labour. Engels provided a framework for this

9   J Hatcher, op cit, p80; D McLellan (ed), *Marx's Grundrisse* (London, 1973), ch17.
10 L Stone, 'Social Mobility in England, 1500-1700', *Past and Present* 33 (1966), p17;
    P Laslett, *The World We Have Lost* (third edition, London, 1983), pp27-36.
11 N Carlin, 'Marxism and the English Civil War', *International Socialism* 10 (1980),
    pp114-115.

investigation: 'From its origin the bourgeoisie was saddled with its anti-thesis: capitalists cannot exist without wage workers', and as small producers developed into a bourgeoisie, so labourers and journeymen developed into a proletariat. He went on to say that 'in every great bourgeois movement there were independent outbursts of that class which was the more or less developed forerunner of the modern proletariat'.[12]

Under the tradition of craft production in manufacture the craftsman or artisan, organised in the guilds and companies, served an apprenticeship and then worked as a wage earning journeyman until he could accumulate the resources to rent a workshop, purchase tools and raw materials, and set up his own business as a small master, himself often employing an apprentice or two and a journeyman. In the 16th century it was 'a reasonable expectation' for most journeymen to establish themselves after a few years as independent small producers with their own workshops, and in fact about four fifths did so, although it took longer for some than others.[13] This may have continued to be the case down to the revolution of the 17th century. Eric Kerridge maintains that in textile manufacture—the most important industry—there was 'an industrial ladder' climbed from apprentice to journeyman, from journeyman to small master with his own loom, and from small master to large master with many looms, employing numerous apprentices, journeymen and servants. He agrees that not all journeymen weavers were successful in becoming their own masters.[14] In London it seems that there was an identity of interests between small masters and journeymen in seeking to defend the earnings of artisans against the merchants who bought their products, and against emerging industrial capitalists who 'offered dangerous competition by hiring cheap labour and dispensing with the egalitarian regulations of the old guild system', threatening the livelihoods of both small masters and journeymen.[15]

Whether or not growing numbers of journeymen remained wage earners all their lives, a general increase in the numbers of wage workers may be posited for areas of agriculture and manufacture falling under capitalist control. Alan Everitt has spoken of the emergence in agriculture before the revolution of 'a growing army of landless, or

12   F Engels, *Socialism: Utopian and Scientific*, op cit, p59.
13   S Rappaport, *Worlds Within Worlds: Structures of Life in 16th Century London* (Cambridge, 1989), pp238-284, 326-376.
14   E Kerridge, *Textile Manufactures in Early Modern England* (Manchester, 1985), pp179-180, 181-182, 183-184, 185-186, 187-189, 190, 191, 193, 197.
15   N Carlin, 'Liberty and Fraternities in the English Revolution: the Politics of London Artisans' Protests, 1635-1659', *International Review of Social History* 39 (1994), pp249-251; K Lindley, *Popular Politics and Religion in Civil War London* (Aldershot, 1997), pp158-165.

almost landless, labourers...dependent on wages alone for their liveli-hood'.[16] Buchanan Sharp has claimed that by the time of the revolution the artisans in the major manufacturing areas of rural England—clothmaking, mining and ironmaking—'depended largely on wages provided by capitalist employers...the skilled as well as unskilled work-force was overwhelmingly propertyless and dependent on wages'.[17]

There is a problem about the proportion of wage earners in the population as a whole. R H Tawney calculated that 'except in those parts of the country...where a large population was employed in tex-tile industries, the family entirely dependent for its livelihood upon wage labour was in rural districts the exception...though the propor-tion of the people employed as wage labourers was growing, the "typ-ical" workman was not a wage labourer, but a small master craftsman or a landholding peasant'.[18] Conservative estimates put the proportion of wage workers at between a quarter and a third of both rural and urban populations. Everitt judges that in Tudor and early Stuart peri-ods 'England still remained an overwhelmingly peasant community: a land of small family farms where outside labour was only occasion-ally employed at peak periods'. Donald Woodward concludes that 'English society during the 16th and early 17th centuries had not yet become a predominantly wage earning society', and A L Beier ob-serves that 'the line between working for wages and being self em-ployed was a fine one: the person who worked purely for cash wages was probably exceptional'.[19]

That last observation introduces the key problem: the number of per-sons in receipt of wages may have been higher or lower than the pro-portions suggested, but the question is, how many were wholly dependent on wages? Many relied on wages for only part of their work-ing lives, as servants and journeymen, or for only part of the year, like the small peasants who provided seasonal labour for the larger farmers. Most wage earners were not entirely dependent on wages for their livelihood: they had a little land and/or rights to pasture a few animals on the common lands, where they could also take wood or dig peat for

16 A Everitt, 'Farm Labourers', in J Thirsk (ed), *The Agrarian History of England and Wales*, vol IV (Cambridge, 1967), pp398-399.
17 B Sharp, *In Contempt of all Authority: Rural Artisans and Riot in the West of England, 1586-1660* (Berkeley, 1980), pp156-174, 257-260.
18 R H Tawney, 'The Assessment of Wages in England by the Justices of the Peace', in W E Minchinton (ed), *Wage Regulation in Pre-Industrial England* (Newton Abbot, 1972), pp63, 65.
19 A Everitt, op cit, pp398-400; D Woodward, 'Wage Rates and Living Standards in Pre-Industrial England', *Past and Present* 91 (1981), pp39-42, 44-45; A L Beier, *Masterless Men: the Vagrancy Problem in England 1560-1640* (London, 1985), p26.

fuel (ie common rights). There was a narrow, perhaps indistinguishable, line between the small farmer who supplemented the resources of his land with wage labour for larger farmers, and the farm labourer who supplemented his wages with the resources of a small plot of land and/or common rights. Many small farmers, notably in pastoral and forested regions, added to their resources by working part of their time in various manufactures, and many artisans in manufactures eked out their wages with the resources from the possession of some land and/or common rights.[20] Gramsci and Shanin located most of these categories of wage earners socially and ideologically with the peasantry: the former described agricultural labourers as 'for the most part simply peasants without land...and not the workers of an agricultural industry developed through concentration of capital and the division of labour'; the latter accounted 'an agricultural labourer lacking a fully fledged farm' and a rural craftsman who had little or no land, but whose employment was provided by agriculture, as marginally 'peasants'.[21] But Lenin related all these categories of wage earners to a developing proletariat, describing them as 'semi-proletarians, or dwarf peasants, ie those who obtain their livelihood partly as wage labourers in agricultural and industrial capitalist enterprises and partly by working their own, or rented, plots of land, which provide only a part of the means of subsistence for their families', adding that 'the lot of these semi-proletarians is a very hard one'.[22] All these considerations will need to be borne in mind when the role of a proletariat in the English Revolution comes under review in the following chapters of this book.

The retention by small peasants, artisans and labourers of some land and common rights underpinned the survival and continuation of the traditional economy and society. The supplement of wage labour in agriculture or manufacture enabled independent smallholding peasants to survive, and agrarian resources allowed artisans to retain a degree of independence because they were not wholly reliant on wages.

The 'putting out system' in manufacture, by which a merchant put out work to a small producer, such as weaving, or a larger producer put out work to a smaller one, such as spinning, reduced the independence

20   D Woodward, op cit, pp44-45; E Kerridge, op cit, pp176-178, 187-192; J M Neeson, *Commoners: Common Right, Enclosure and Social Change in England 1700-1820* (Cambridge, 1996), pp297-319.
21   Q Hoare and G Nowell-Smith (eds), *Selections from the Prison Notebooks of Antonio Gramsci* (London, 1971), p75; T Shanin (ed), *Peasants and Peasant Societies* (Harmondsworth, 1971), pp15-16.
22   V I Lenin, 'Preliminary Draft of Theses on the Agrarian Question', *Selected Works*, vol II (2 vols, London, 1947), pp645-646.

of the small producer, but did not make him into a wage earner. It is difficult to discern the point at which the small producer was transformed into a proletarian.

The small producer in manufacture who became dependent on a merchant, who provided him with his raw materials and paid him for his finished product, is often regarded as equivalent to a wage worker, de facto a wage worker.[23] Albert Soboul, in his study of *sans-culottes* in the French Revolution, differentiated between the 'independent craftsman' and the 'dependent craftsman'. The latter headed his own concern, possessed his own tools and machines, and hired labour. He appeared to be an employer but was really a wage earner, according to Soboul, 'strictly dependent upon the merchant who supplies him with the raw material and who distributes the finished article'.[24] However, the 'dependent craftsman' still possessed his own workshop and instruments of production, he was the patriarchal master of his workforce, he controlled his own time and methods of work, and he owned the product of his labour. Soboul himself made the point that he did not regard himself as a wage worker but identified himself with the independent small producers.[25] But when the artisan was tied to a single merchant-manufacturer who put work out to him, and he contracted to supply an article for a fixed sum of money, it is argued that he was employed at a piece rate wage, and that he had ceased to own the product of his labour but sold his labour power itself.[26] On the other hand he still possessed the means of production, and it may be argued that he did not sell his labour power but contracted to provide a service, though in this case not for the personal consumption of the purchaser but for the latter to dispose of in trade.[27] Capitalism remained external to the process of production, which was, as Marx observed, a continuation of the pre-capitalist mode, and although Marx did describe producers under the 'putting out system' as wage workers, that was not in the context of the capitalist mode. The capitalist did not take possession of the means of production, and he did not

---

23 C Lis and H Soly, *Poverty and Capitalism in Pre-Industrial Europe* (Atlantic Highlands, 1979), p217.

24 A Soboul, *The Parisian Sans-Culottes and the French Revolution 1793-94*, translated by G Lewis (Oxford, 1964), pp51-52.

25 D Goodman and M Redclift, *From Peasant to Proletarian: Capitalist Development and Agrarian Transition* (Oxford, 1981), pp85-93, 96-98.

26 E Lipson, *The Economic History of England*, vol II (fifth edition, London, 1948), ppxxvi-xxvii; I Wallerstein, *The Modern World System*, vol II (New York, 1980), p195; M Gould, *Revolution in the Development of Capitalism: The Coming of the English Revolution* (Berkeley, 1987), pp155-156.

27 E Kerridge, op cit, pp181,191.

take control of the organisation of the work.[28] Proletarianisation 'moves workers from a position of control over the organisation of their work to one in which that organisation is imposed from outside. At its most fundamental, the rise of a modern working class is the saga of power in the workshops, and proletarianisation is the process that deprives workers of their power'.[29] Under the 'putting out system' the small producer lost some of this independence but he was not fully proletarianised.

The crucial issue for Marx was possession of the means of production, which did not cover just tools or machines but also the organisation of production and working conditions.[30] 'On the whole, the labourer and his means of production remained closely united' under the 'putting out system', said Marx, 'like the snail with its shell'. The full development of capitalism would be marked by the proto-capitalist becoming the owner of the means of production and the appropriator of the surplus labour of the producers, who would become the creators of his capital and make him fully a capitalist. Proletarianisation was a dual process in which the means of production were separated from the producer and became capital confronting him, and the producer had only his labour power, which became a commodity that he sold on the market to the capitalist.[31] This was happening at the time of the English Revolution, for Thomas Hobbes, the philosopher, observed that labour was 'a commodity exchanged for benefit' and that 'poor people sell their labour'.[32]

Marx's explanation of the transition from feudalism to capitalism centred on the dispossessing of small producers (peasant and artisan) from the means of production. His view will be quoted at length because it contains a thesis about property which will be explored in the next section. He refers to small producers as 'labourers' and to the means of production as the 'means of labour':

28   K Marx, *Capital*, vol III, op cit, pp334-335; C Middleton, 'Women's Labour and the Transition to Pre-Industrial Capitalism', in L Charles and L Duffin (eds), *Women and Work in Pre-Industrial England* (London, 1985), p194; J Merrington, 'Town and Country in the Transition to Capitalism', in R H Hilton (ed), *The Transition from Feudalism to Capitalism*, op cit, pp189-190.

29   T M Safley and L N Rosenband (eds), *The Workplace Before the Factory: Artisans and Proletarians 1500-1800* (Ithaca, 1993), pp6-7, 10.

30   G V Plekhanov, *In Defence of Materialism*, translated by A Rothstein (London, 1947), p147.

31   D McLellan (ed), op cit, ch 17; K Marx, *Capital*, vol I, op cit, p339; F Engels, *Socialism: Utopian and Scientific*, op cit, pp101,111; R Brenner, 'Bourgeois Revolution and Transition to Capitalism', in A L Beier, D Cannadine and J M Rosenheim (eds), *The First Modern Society* (Cambridge, 1989), pp292-294.

32   T Hobbes, *Leviathan*, edited by M Oakeshott, (Oxford), p161; T Hobbes, *Behemoth or The Long Parliament*, edited by F Tönnies (second edition, London, 1969), p126.

What does the primitive accumulation of capital, ie its historical genesis, resolve itself into?... It only means the expropriation of the immediate producers, ie the dissolution of private property based on the labour of its owner... The private property of the labourer in his means of production is the foundation of petty industry, whether agricultural, manufacturing, or both... Of course, this petty mode of production exists also under slavery, serfdom, and other states of dependence. But it flourishes, it lets loose its whole energy, it attains its adequate classical form, only where the labourer is the private owner of his own means of labour set in action by himself: the peasant of the land which he cultivates, the artisan of the tool which he handles... The expropriation of the great mass of the people from the soil, from the means of subsistence, and from the means of labour, this fearful and painful expropriation of the mass of the people forms the prelude to the history of capital... Self earned private property...is supplanted by capitalistic private property, which rests on exploitation of the nominally free labour of others, ie on wage labour.[33]

Resistance to proletarianisation

Marx saw the transition as extending in England from the 15th to the 18th century. The resistance of small producers to this process, which may be rightly termed a class struggle, was sustained throughout this period, including being a key element in the English Revolution. Marx's account needs to be modified by noting that peasants were often successful in resisting increased demands from their lords, and small peasants, artisans and labourers 'often fought a very successful class struggle' against both feudal landlords and village bourgeoisie to secure for some time the survival of many smallholdings and common rights. Landless or near landless peasants struggled to retain their common rights in order to avoid becoming completely dependent on wages and losing their independent way of life.[34]

The agitations amongst the rank and file of the London guilds and companies in the 1640s and 1650s were a major element in the revolution. Sometimes they referred to their support for parliament in the civil war and sometimes they invoked radical political principles.

33 K Marx, *Capital*, vol I, op cit, pp667-714.
34 H Medick, 'The Transition from Feudalism to Capitalism', in R Samuel (ed), *People's History and Socialist Theory* (London, 1981), p124; J M Neeson, op cit, pp81, 106-109, 177-178, 259-293; C E Searle, op cit, pp131-132.

These were not, as Margaret James thought, struggles between 'a growing class of wage earners' and their employers, but struggles by small producers in defence of their independence. Some producers enlarged their operations by increasing their labour force, taking on more apprentices than permitted under the rules of the companies and employing unapprenticed labour, and so developing towards becoming capitalist manufacturers. Tailors protested in 1649 that 'divers rich men of our trade by taking over great multitudes of apprentices do weaken the poorer sort of us', and printers complained that 'some few of the rich' masters 'oppress the lesser printers...by keeping large numbers of apprentices'. The focal point of the struggles in the London companies was the demand of small masters for the enforcement of the regulations which required a seven year apprenticeship and set limits to the number of apprentices a master might employ. The intention was to prevent larger masters from taking work away from small masters, who would then be liable to lose their independent businesses and have to work for the larger producers. Small masters might be driven out of their craft altogether and have to seek unskilled labouring jobs. London weavers said that 'at the beginning of the war many of us and our servants engaged for the parliament', but when 'we returned to follow our callings, we can get no employment', so that many hundreds were driven to become 'porters, labourers, water bearers, chimney sweepers, salt criers and coalmen'.[35] The decline of guild control was a precondition for the development of industrial capitalism, and the fact that the enforcement of guild or company regulations was an issue in the 1640s and 1650s points to the transition to capitalism being an issue in the revolution. But the guilds were unable to control the expansion of manufacturing in the suburbs of London.[36]

The dispossession of peasants and artisans from the means of production was a precondition for capitalist development but, paradoxically, the survival of an agrarian base for many farm labourers and manufacturing workers also facilitated capitalist development. Smallholders provided a reservoir of labour for capitalist farmers and capitalist manufacturers, furnishing them with a supply of labour which could be readily contracted or expanded in response to movements of

35 M James, *Social Problems and Policy during the Puritan Revolution* (London, 1930), pp192-223; G Unwin, *Industrial Organisation in the 16th and 17th Centuries* (1904, reprinted in London, 1957), pp197,199, 207-208; N Carlin, 'Liberty and Fraternities', op cit, pp237-251.
36 A L Beier, 'Engine of Manufacture: the Trades of London', in A L Beier and R Finlay (eds), *London 1500-1700: The Making of the Metropolis* (London, 1986), pp157-159.

the market, and at a lower cost because they were not wholly dependent on wages for their subsistence. The increasing numbers dependent for part or all of their livelihood on money wages, low as they were, injected modest additions of purchasing power into the economy and so contributed to the self sustaining growth of the home market, which was another precondition for capitalist development.[37]

The distinction must be emphasised between the class of independent small producers (generally termed at the time the 'middle sort of people') and the class of full time wage labourers (generally included under the designation 'the poor'). The former comprised peasants who owned or rented a farm which was sufficient for their subsistence without having to resort to working for wages to any major extent or at all, and artisans who possessed their own workshops, raw materials and tools. It was from amongst the class of independent small producers that the main driving force of the revolution probably came, and amongst whom the radicals certainly found their chief strength. But revolutions commonly begin with alliances between diverse social groups against an existing regime, and as the revolution develops the different and conflicting interests of these groups emerge. In the English Revolution opposition to Charles I and the royalists brought together a few aristocrats, some gentry and merchants, numerous farmers and artisans as well as labourers, leading historians to jump to the conclusion that it was not a class struggle. But it was with the progress of the revolution that class differences and class conflicts emerged, shaping the course and outcome of the revolution.[38]

In the present context the proposition is that initially in the English Revolution there was cooperation between radical elements of the 'middle sort' and rebellious elements of the labouring poor. Early on it was observed in the anti-royalist riots of 1642 that 'this fury was not only in the rabble, but many of the better sort behaved themselves as if there had been a dissolution of all government'.[39] The gulf between small producers and their workers was not great, at least economically. Richard Baxter wrote of cloth manufacture at Kidderminster in Worcestershire, where he was minister, 'Three or four of the richest thriving masters of the trade got but £500 or £600 in 20 years,

37 H Medick, op cit, p124; C Lis and H Soly, op cit, pp150-151; D Goodman and M Redclift, op cit, pp24, 53-54, 62-63, 71, 95; M Gould, op cit, p165; A D Lublinskaya, *French Absolutism: the Crucial Phase 1620-1629*, translated by B Pearce (Cambridge, 1968), pp55, 68; D Parker, *Class and State in Ancien Regime France: the Road to Modernity?* (London, 1996), p237.
38 K Kautsky, op cit, pp372-373.
39 F Peck, *Desiderata Curiosa*, vol II, book xii (London, 1735), pp23-25.

and it may be lose £100 of it at once to an ill debtor. The generality of the master workmen lived but a little better than their journeymen (from hand to mouth), but only that they laboured not altogether so hard'.[40] The 'middle sort', where they were strong enough, gave leadership to the poor. John Corbet, a minister in Gloucestershire, recorded the support of the 'middle sort' there for parliament in the civil war, notably in the cloth manufacturing districts, and said that 'the poor and needy...observed those men by whom those manufactures were maintained that kept them alive'.[41] The common action of 'middle' and 'poorer' sorts may have been rooted in shared antagonism towards the ruling class, as expressed by Laurence Clarkson, a tailor, in 1647:

> For who are the oppressors, but the nobility and gentry; and who are oppressed, is not the yeoman, the farmer, the tradesman, and the labourer? Then consider, have you not chosen oppressors to redeem you from oppression?... It is naturally inbred in the major part of the nobility and gentry...to judge the poor but fools, and themselves wise, and therefore when you the commonalty call a parliament, they are confident such must be chosen that are noblest and richest...but...reason affirms...these are not your equals, neither are these sensible of the burden that lies upon you; for indeed...your slavery is their liberty, your poverty is their prosperity.[42]

The question, however, will have to be explored subsequently of how far such alliance was sustainable in the face of divergent class interests between small producers and wage workers.

Small producers as peasants were driven by anxiety to retain their land, and as artisans by concern to avoid becoming dependent on wealthy merchants, and both groups by fear of being reduced to wage workers. The radicals developed an ideology that the producer had property in his own labour and its fruits. This expressed the class consciousness of small producers in their struggle with the ruling class and its institutions, for it proclaimed that the rent of the landlord, the tithes paid to the church, and the taxes levied by the state were appropriated from the labours of the producers, and this was sanctioned and enforced by the coercion of the law. The wealth of the rich, they said, was created by the labours of the poor. The Buckinghamshire Levellers declared,

40 M Sylvester (ed), *Reliquiae Baxterianae* (London, 1696), p94.
41 J Corbet, *An Historicall Relation of the Military Government of Gloucester* (London, 1645), p9.
42 Quoted in P Zagorin, *A History of Political Thought in the English Revolution* (1954, reprinted in Bristol, 1997), p31.

'When a man has got bread, viz: necessaries by his labour, it is his bread', and he should not have to pay 'tribute out of his labour' in rents and dues to a landlord who does not work for it. The rulers 'do likewise extort away the labours of their poor brethren, and take out the bread out of their mouths, and from their poor wives and children, by their unreasonable, unlawful, unjust and wicked' taxes and tithes 'as that the flour of those industrious men's labours are boulted out from them, and only the bran left them to feed on'.[43] A manifesto of 1647 against tithes declared, 'We have a natural right unto our goods gotten by the daily labour of our hands, and so we have a right unto our crop of corn, as it is the fruit of our proper stock of money and year's labour'.[44]

Marx saw this doctrine, that the small producer had property in his own labour, as arising from the petty mode of production, of which the defining characteristic was that the small producer owned the means of production as his property.[45] C B Macpherson, however, argued that this doctrine arose from the development of capitalism and provided a conception of property appropriate to the establishment of 'a full capitalist market society', because the notion that the producer owned his labour implied that he could sell his labour, and so suited the capitalist mode of production which regarded labour as a commodity.[46] Macpherson's formulation, that 'the free alienation of property, including the property in one's labour, by sale and purchase is an essential element of capitalist production', ignores Marx's qualification that what the worker sells is not his labour but his labour power, and confuses the selling of labour with the selling of the fruits of labour. The small producers resisted the fruits of their labour being taken from them and the Levellers defended private property, because it protected the small producers' ownership of the means of production.[47]

The livelihood of the craftsman or artisan depended on the difference between his costs of production and the price at which he could sell his wares. Many craftsmen and artisans, rather than selling directly to the consumer, were selling increasingly to merchants for retail or export:

43   G H Sabine (ed), *The Works of Gerrard Winstanley* (1941, reprinted in New York, 1965), pp627-628, 633-634; W Haller and G Davies (eds), *The Leveller Tracts* (1944, reprinted in Gloucester, Massachusetts, 1964), p439.
44   Quoted in C Hill, *Economic Problems of the Church* (Oxford, 1956), p156.
45   K Marx, *Capital*, vol I, op cit, pp713-715.
46   C B Macpherson, *The Political Theory of Possessive Individualism* (Oxford, 1962), pp148-154, 214-220; C B Macpherson, *Democratic Theory* (Oxford, 1973), pp129-133.
47   D M Wolfe (ed), *Leveller Manifestoes of the Puritan Revolution* (1944, reprinted in London, 1967), pp288, 390-391; D B Robertson, *The Religious Foundations of Leveller Democracy* (New York, 1951), p87.

It is very strange to my understanding, that one man should do the work, and another man receive the wages; I mean, that the honest clothier who has toiled much in the making of his cloth, shall not have the benefit to sell it here for his own gain…but…must make sale to them, in whose power it is to give him what price they please, whereby he is cheated of the fruits of his labour.[48]

London artisans during the revolution addressed class conscious manifestos to the rich merchants of the city:

When with extreme care, racked credit, and hard labour ourselves and servants have produced our manufactures, with what cruelty have you wrought, and still work upon our necessities, and enrich yourselves upon our extremities, offering yea frequently buying our work for less than (you know) the stuff whereof it was made cost us; by which the like unconscionable means in grinding the faces of the poor, and advancing yourselves on our ruins, most of you rich citizens come to your wealth.[49]

You of the city that buy our work must have your tables furnished and your cups overflow; and therefore will give us little or nothing for our work, even what you please, because you know we must sell for monies to set our families on work, or else we famish. Thus our flesh is that whereupon you rich men live, and wherewith you deck and adorn yourselves.[50]

These radicals were not speaking for wage labourers but for small producers, who sold the fruits of their labour, not their labour power itself. They were not employees but employers—the references in the manifestos to 'servants' and 'families' (the latter term denoted 'households' and so included living-in servants and apprentices) indicate that they employed apprentices and journeymen. The merchant was taking a middleman's profit, as the intermediary between producer and consumer, and incurred the odium that middlemen traditionally attracted. The independence of the producer was being reduced by cutting him off from the market both for his raw materials and for the distribution of his finished goods, and the conflict was between small manufacturing producers and merchants.[51] A manifesto of the printers asserted the value of small producers above that of merchants:

For without the clothier what were the drapier, without the hatmaker

---

48 T Johnson, *Plea for Free-Men's Liberties* (1646).
49 *Englands Troublers Troubled* (1648).
50 D M Wolfe (ed), op cit, pp275-276.
51 R H Hilton, *Class Conflict and the Crisis of Feudalism*, op cit, pp83-84; M Dobb, *Studies in the Development of Capitalism* (London, 1946), p7.

where were the haberdasher, and without the printer where were the bookseller? Yea, having the clothier what need (necessarily) is there of the draper...and having the printer there is no fear of wanting books though there were no bookseller.[52]

The most common unit of production was the family. Most production in agriculture and industry took place within the household of small farmers or artisans. The household often included living-in servants and apprentices who, together with wives and children, formed the workforce. It was a patriarchal institution, presided over by the father, who managed the business and disciplined his wife, children, servants and apprentices.[53] At the base of the economic system, male heads of households exploited the labour of their wives, children, servants and apprentices. De Ste Croix raises the question whether women, or wives, formed 'a distinct economic class', though he comes to the conclusion that their class position was more importantly determined by belonging to a peasant or artisan household.[54] The concept of 'surplus labour' is not intended to apply to the production of food or goods for consumption by the producers themselves. Female labour in so far as it is a contribution to the household economy is 'necessary labour'. But, says Chris Middleton, 'it is all too easy to slide into the false assumption that the "value" of women's labour can be measured solely in terms of what they provide for their households and families... It is possible for women's labour to be expropriated by their husbands, fathers, brothers and so on', for instance, when their labour increases the production of the household for the market and provides its male head with a surplus over and above the mere subsistence of the family.[55] But amongst the poor, wives were often independent wage earners, and the household was sustained by two wage packets.[56]

The labour of children played an important part in the economies of farmers and artisans—from the age of eight in agriculture and even earlier in industry, at six or seven in textile manufacture, or even four or five.[57] As exploited labour their position was the same as that of

52   Quoted by G Unwin, op cit, p212.
53   C Hill, 'The Poor and the People in 17th Century England', in F Krantz (ed), *History from Below: Studies in Popular Protest and Popular Ideology* (Oxford, 1988), pp38-39; S Amussen, *An Ordered Society: Gender and Class in Early Modern England* (Oxford, 1988), pp68, 70, 94.
54   G E M de Ste Croix, *The Class Struggle in the Ancient Greek World* (1981; third impression London, 1997), pp100-101; R Browning, 'The Class Struggle in Ancient Greece', *Past and Present* 100 (1983), p151.
55   C Middleton, op cit, pp187-188.
56   R A Houlbrooke, *The English Family 1450-1700* (London, 1984), pp106-109.
57   Ibid, pp127, 153-154.

wives, providing 'necessary labour' for the household or 'surplus labour' if contributing to production over and above subsistence of the household. The master craftsmen were the exploiters of the labour of apprentices: 'the apprentice as a labourer who was paid no wages, or very low wages, during the period between the end of his training in the craft and the formal end of the apprenticeship' had ceased to be simply a trainee and had become 'an exploited labourer in receipt of his subsistence only'. The masters relied on the merchant oligarchies who governed the towns 'to keep their employees (apprentices and journeymen) in order' and to protect them from discontented apprentices and journeymen.[58]

Divergence between small producers and wage workers

The degree of independence of the small producers varied: a few peasants and craftsmen were advancing to become capitalists, notably by extending production for the market by means of the employment of more wage labour, and others were sinking into wage workers. Petty production contained within itself 'the embryo of capitalist relations'.[59] This raises the question of whether the small producers could develop clear class consciousness and effective class action.[60] There was an ambiguity in their position. As owners of the means of production they were exploiters of labour and thus had something in common with larger exploiters of labour, like landlords and merchants, but as manual workers directly engaged in production and themselves exploited by landlords or merchants, they had sympathy with the wage dependent poor who suffered oppression. Classes are always changing and the class of small producers was splitting between those hopeful of rising to become larger owners and bigger employers, and those fearful of being forced down into wage workers. 'The germs both of proletarian and industrial capitalist class consciousness were already contained in the craftsmen', wrote Kautsky.[61] It is a decisive factor in the English Revolution that the 'middle sort' was divided between elements that favoured developments which we see now as facilitating the

58 R H Hilton, *Class Conflict and the Crisis of Feudalism*, op cit, pp83-84, 109, 215.

59 M Dobb, *Studies...*, op cit, p20.

60 K Marx, 'The Eighteenth Brumaire of Louis Bonaparte', in K Marx and F Engels, *Selected Works*, vol I, op cit, pp302-303; G Lukács, op cit, pp55-62; K Kautsky, op cit, pp252-253; G Rudé, *Ideology and Popular Protest* (London, 1980), p27; R H Hilton, *The English Peasantry in the Later Middle Ages* (Oxford, 1975), ch I, 'The Peasantry as a Class'.

61 K Kautsky, op cit, pp252-253, 367.

growth of capitalism and elements hostile towards those developments. The revolution was a crucial phase in crystallising a proto-bourgeoisie and a proto-proletariat.

The landless poor migrated to areas where there were extensive commons and wastes. The wastes were uncultivated lands between villages that provided rough common grazing. These migrants squatted on the wastes and built themselves cottages or cabins illegally, or landlords took land out of the wastes and erected cottages for rent to the migrants. The attractions for the migrants were the resources of the commons and wastes on which they could pasture a few animals, and from which they could take building materials and fuel. Another attraction was the existence of local industry in which they could obtain employment, and the increase of population on the wastes drew in new industries seeking to take advantage of the availability of plentiful and cheap labour. These squatters and cottagers were thus able to find some sort of livelihood, poor and precarious as it was, by combining petty farming with wage labour in industry. But the established farmers in the villages, both small and large farmers, found that their traditional resources in the commons and wastes for pasture, wood, peat, and water were being eroded by the competition of the new settlers, who had little or no land of their own but lived off the commons and wastes. They complained that where 'houses are set up without ground to the same and lie upon any common by continuance, they take common without right and so prejudice the other rightful commoners'. They alleged that the settlers were beggars, idlers and thieves, and brought up their children to like ways. But, viewed in another way, the commons and wastes were not nurseries of crime, but the means 'through which the labouring poor preserved a measure of independence and self respect'. The established farmers blamed the situation on those who made profit from the influx of the poor—the landlords who increased their incomes by building cottages on the wastes for rent or split existing tenancies into cottage holdings, and the cloth manufacturers, mine owners and ironmasters who wanted supplies of cheap casual labour. But the established farmers themselves could also make profit by subletting cottages, or providing building plots, or taking in lodgers:

> In the earlier part of the 16th century the interests of smallholders and cottagers were not sharply distinguished, but the process of social differentiation together with the pressure of population on the diminishing resources of pasture, fuel, and living space widened the gulf between these social groups... Increasingly in the early 17th century,

smallholders were prepared to cooperate in attempts to exclude cottagers and squatters from commons by means of enclosure agreements, disafforestation, fen draining schemes, or by simply destroying cottages that offended them.[62]

Capitalist industrial development caused some rural communities to adapt to industrial society, and landlords and farmers to cooperate in profiting from the change. On Cannock Chase in Staffordshire there was considerable development of iron founding, charcoal burning and metal working, and cottages were erected on the wastes and messuages were subdivided for lease to under-tenants, in order to house the workforce. In 1606 Lord Paget, the leading landlord, entered into an agreement with 139 of his tenants to compose past differences by rationalising tenures and instituting a body of manorial customs regulating the economic rights of lord and tenant. This 'reflected the significant social changes that rural industry and the influx of artisans had brought to Cannock Chase':

> Whatever differences had divided the Pagets and their tenants in the past, the cleavage was now between those who possessed land and the virtually landless craftsmen. By settling their differences concerning tenures, rents, and manorial customs, both Lord Paget and his copyhold tenants could get on with the business of leasing cottages and small plots of land to the artisans. From what we know of subleasing to under-tenants elsewhere, all stood to make substantial profits.[63]

At Whickham in County Durham in the first half of the 17th century there was a considerable development of coal mining. There was 'a head on collision between the rights claimed by the coal owners and those defended by the copyholders' (tenants who held their land according to the customs of the manor). Cottages proliferated on the commons in order to provide labour for the coal industry, but copyholders proved willing to hive off cottages and building plots; the increased population of the coalfield provided them with a ready market for grain, meat and dairy produce; they supplied horses, oxen, oats and hay to the coal masters; and they profited by providing wains for transport of the coal. 'In the late 16th century the manor of Whickham

62 R B Manning, *Village Revolts: Social Protest and Popular Disturbances in England,
    1509-1640* (Oxford, 1988), pp140-142, 170-172, 176-178, 256-257; B Sharp, *In
    Contempt of All Authority*, op cit, pp158-165; B Sharp, 'Common Rights, Charities, and
    the Disorderly Poor', in G Eley and W Hunt (eds), *Reviving the English Revolution*
    (London, 1988), pp113-116, 124-126; S Hindle, 'Persuasion and Protest in the
    Cuddington Common Enclosure Dispute 1635-1639', *Past and Present* 158 (1998), p71.
63 R B Manning, op cit, pp140-142.

had been an agricultural community partially involved in industrial activity', but by the mid-17th century the copyholders had adapted themselves to an emerging industrial order, and 'the Elizabethan agrarian community had been submerged within a larger industrial and commercial order'.[64]

The dividing line between small producer and proletarian was the possession or not of the means of production, and for many poor peasants and artisans this involved whether or not they had some land and/or common rights. Struggles against enclosures of commons and wastes continued throughout the revolution. The enclosure of land involved the abolition of common rights over it and 'the appropriation to one person of land which had previously been at the disposal of the whole community'.[65] The leaders of the revolution came down in favour of enclosures:

> The not unsurprising decision of the House of Commons (whose earlier attack on enclosure in the *Grand Remonstrance* had raised popular hopes) to throw their weight behind enclosure after 1643 ensured that enclosure rioters did not form a radical agrarian wing of the parliamentarian cause.[66]

This was a pointer to an underlying trend in the parliamentarian party towards capitalism, and it reflected the changed attitude of the better off peasant farmers who were evolving into capitalist farmers. Landlords obtained the agreement of their more substantial tenants to enclosure schemes by offering them leases of parcels of the newly enclosed waste on favourable terms. The substantial tenants could sublease the waste they obtained at enclosure in small parcels to the poor and thus realise many times the amount they themselves paid in rent to the lord, and so tenants shared with the lord the profits of exploiting the poor. 'The fear of poor persons squatting or being settled upon the waste was often as strong a motive for the more prosperous tenants to acquiesce in enclosure as the financial inducements... Thus the social cleavage was not between lord and tenant but rather between lord and tenants on the one hand, and cottagers and landless persons on the other.' Buchanan Sharp maintains:

---

64 D Levine and K Wrightson, *The Making of an Industrial Society: Whickham 1560-1765* (Oxford, 1991), pp106-151.

65 J Thirsk (ed), *The Agrarian History of England and Wales*, vol IV (Cambridge, 1967), pp200-201.

66 K Lindley, *Fenland Riots and the English Revolution* (London, 1982), ch 5; B Sharp, *In Contempt of all Authority*, op cit, pp250-256; J Morrill and J Walter, 'Order and Disorder in the English Revolution', in A Fletcher and J Stevenson (eds), *Order and Disorder in Early Modern England* (Cambridge, 1985), p140.

The better sort began to distance themselves from the poor in a variety of ways including acceptance of enclosure as a positive social good that would eliminate, if not poverty, at least the attractiveness of their parishes to the poor. Limiting access to commons would enable control to be exercised over the poor. Elimination of the waste would prevent an increase in the number of idle and disorderly poor.

At enclosure the lords of manors and their tenants—yeomen and husbandmen—were amply compensated for their own loss of common rights by allotments of the enclosed land. But smallholders, landless cottagers and rural artisans were inadequately compensated for their loss of access to the commons and wastes, or not at all, and lost their cushion against dependence on wage labour. John Walter writes of a reordering of the relationships of the 'middling sort' with other social groups. The larger farmers ceased to resist enclosure, 'as long as it accommodated their interests', because 'agrarian capitalism' was becoming the foundation of 'their growing wealth and power'. Seen from the other side, by J M Neeson, enclosure tore away the mask of shared interests and revealed the different interests of poorer and richer villagers; it brought about a growing separation of classes and taught the smallholders and landless labourers, who 'lost their winter fuel, the grazing for a cow or a few sheep, the feed for pigs and geese', 'the new reality of class relations' of an emerging village bourgeoisie and proletariat: 'Enclosure had a terrible but instructive visibility.' This may be illustrated by the agreement which the tenants of Sutton in the Isle of Ely reached with their lord, the dean and chapter of Ely, for the division and enclosure of their fen common. In the fenland right of common was denied to newly built cottages, but the tenants of Sutton had connived at these cottagers exercising right of common in the fen, 'otherwise they would go abegging'. The tenants were allotted 14 acres each of the common, plus one acre for every two acres they had in the arable lands of the village. It was proposed that each new cottage should receive two acres, but this was defeated in favour of increasing the shares of the tenants and giving the cottagers only the use of a small common. The cottagers protested that they had been overridden by the power of their rich neighbours.[67] Nevertheless, ambiguity persisted, for bigger farmers, who paid the largest proportion of the poor rates, might still oppose enclosure because they feared that the loss of common rights would reduce their poorer neighbours to dependence on

67   R B Manning, op cit, pp110, 115, 127-129; B Sharp, 'Common Rights, Charities, and the Disorderly Poor', op cit, pp113-118, 126-127; J Walter, 'A Rising of the People? The Oxfordshire Rising of 1596', *Past and Present* 107 (1985), pp120-122; J M Neeson, 'The Opponents of Enclosure in 18th Century Northamptonshire', *Past and Present* 105

poor relief. During the revolution, partly as a response to popular revolts and partly out of fear of strengthening the radical movements such as the Levellers, Diggers and Fifth Monarchists, efforts were made to reduce the adverse impact of enclosures on the poor and to remedy some of their complaints.[68]

The 'middle sort', writes John Walter, 'approached the revolution Janus faced. They were concerned to defend their property and faith against royal absolutism and episcopal Arminianism and, for some, to assert their social status against the old elite. But they were also anxious not to see these threatened from below':

> Those who sided with parliament (and we should not assume that there was a natural identity between the 'middling sort' and support for parliament) wished for political and religious reform, not least to strengthen their position over their poor neighbours. But they did not seek the radical social and economic reforms that the poorer sort might have sought.[69]

The caveat in parenthesis seems redundant to this persuasive statement of the outlook of the 'middling sort' who 'sided with parliament'.

The Levellers said little about wage labourers. One of the few references in their manifestos was a call that 'care be taken forthwith to advance the native commodities of this nation, that the poor may have better wages for their labour, and that manufactures may be increased'.[70] These phrases are significant, for they expressed the demand of the radicals in general for the poor to be set to work, which reflected a shift promoted by the revolutionaries from regarding the poor as a burden on the community—on the 'middle sort' who had to pay poor rates for their relief—to regarding them as a potential asset which could be employed to increase the production of manufactures.[71] That, as one pamphlet said, would enrich the nation 'by encouraging all their labour and industry, advancing home made commodities' whose export could thus

(1984), pp138-139; K Lindley, *Fenland Riots*, op cit, pp40, 142-143; C Holmes, 'Drainers and Fenmen: the Problem of Popular Political Consciousness in the 17th Century', in A Fletcher and J Stevenson (eds), op cit, pp193-194; S Hindle, op cit, pp69-76.

68   J Thirsk, 'Agrarian Problems in the English Revolution', in R C Richardson (ed), *Town and Countryside in the English Revolution* (Manchester, 1992).

69   J Walter, 'The Impact on Society: a World Turned Upside Down?', in J Morrill (ed), *The Impact of the English Civil War* (London, 1991), pp120-121; J Morrill and J Walter, op cit, pp152-153.

70   D M Wolfe (ed), op cit, p270.

71   C Webster, *The Great Instauration: Science, Medicine and Reform 1626-1660* (London, 1975), pp361-362, 455-456; J O Appleby, *Economic Thought and Ideology in 17th Century England* (Princeton, 1978), ch 6; C Lis and H Soly, op cit, p127.

be increased many times over in a few years.[72] 'The wealth and strength of all countries are in the poor,' wrote Peter Chamberlen in 1649, 'for they do all the great and necessary works... The poor are by far the greatest part of the commonwealth...[and] the only riches of a commonwealth is by employing the poor and making such industrious as are not.' Chamberlen concluded by calling on all men, and especially statesmen, 'to look no more upon the poor as a burden, but as the richest treasure of a nation, if orderly and well employed'.[73] This policy sprang in part from humanitarian concern for the poor but it was conducive to the development of capitalist enterprise.

For the Levellers and other radicals the law relating to debt was a more pressing problem than wages. The difficulties of recovering money from those who could afford to pay, and the sufferings in prison of those who could not afford to pay, were close to the hearts of small producers, for they were constantly involved both in giving credit and in borrowing money to stock their farms or workshops.[74] It must be borne in mind that many of the 'middle sort' were employers of labour and had an interest in keeping wages down. Real wages may have increased during the 1650s.[75] Amidst all the complaints about wages being too low, there were those in this period who protested that they were too high: the wages of servants 'being advanced to such an extraordinary height, that they are likely ere long to be masters and their masters servants, many poor husbandmen being forced to pay as much to their servants for wages as to their landlords for rent'. The grand jury of Worcestershire in 1661 represented as a great grievance 'the unreasonableness of servants' wages...so that the servants are grown so proud and idle that the master cannot be known from the servant, except it be because the servant wears better clothes than his master'.[76]

72 *Long Parliament Work* (London, 1659); *Chaos* (London, 1659); W Sprigge, *A Modest Plea, for an Equal Common-Wealth, Against Monarchy* (London, 1659); *England's Safety in the Laws Supremacy* (London, 1659).
73 P Chamberlen, *The Poore Man's Advocate* (London, 1649), pp1, 14, 30.
74 P S Seaver, *Wallington's World: A Puritan Artisan in 17th Century London* (London, 1985), pp123-124; D Veall, *The Popular Movement for Law Reform 1640-1660* (Oxford, 1970), pp12-17, 145-151; B Capp, *The Fifth Monarchy Men* (London, 1972), pp161-168.
75 A L Morton, *A People's History of England* (1938, third edition London, 1989), p219; M Ashley, *Financial and Commercial Policy of the Cromwellian Protectorate* (second edition, London, 1962); J Thirsk (ed), *The Agrarian History of England and Wales*, vol V, part ii (Cambridge, 1985), p879; D Hirst, 'Locating the 1650s in England's 17th Century', *History*, vol 81, No 263 (1996), pp337, 379.
76 R H Tawney, op cit, pp65, 67-68; J Hatcher, op cit, p78.

Resistance by wage labourers

Although one pamphleteer said that 'the only cry of honest poor men is that they want employment',[77] it does appear that 'low wages were more important than unemployment in causing hardship', but poverty was often the result of under-employment (the low number of days of work in the year).[78] Some radicals did speak up for the wage labourers. John Cooke, a barrister who was a counsel for the prosecution at the trial of Charles I, expressed concern that the wages of 'the poor labouring man that has nothing but what he gets by his day labour' were insufficient to feed his family, so that 'he must beg, steal, or starve'. Admittedly he was writing at a time of rising food prices, but he noted the variability of wage earnings, sometimes 3s a week, sometimes 2s, 'and some weeks not 12d'.[79] The famous radical pamphlet *Tyranipocrit* stressed the extreme economic inequalities and the indifference of the well to do for the plight of the poor:

> As for some to have so many hundred pounds a year for doing of nothing, or for executing of some needless office, or to oversee and command others, etc, and a poor labouring man must work for three or four pence a day, and we uncharitable partial wretches can behold all this and be silent, and we pass it over as a matter not worthy of consideration.

'And we will pay them poorly' to till our land, 'and when they have done it, we will esteem them almost so much as we do of our hounds and horses, and yet we will be faithful Christians, and we will rule all Christendom'.[80] Another tract said:

> Those men that have nothing but their labour to subsist on either by ploughing, threshing, hedging, and such like country employments, are little better than slaves. Let them be never so laborious, their wages is so little, that they are never in all their lives able to lay up anything for the subsistence of their families after their death; and therefore it generally comes to pass, that if country labourers die while their children are young and unable to work for themselves, they must unavoidably be relieved by the alms of the parish, which as the laws are executed is sad livelihood.[81]

77 P Chamberlen, op cit, p20.
78 A L Beier, 'Poverty and Progress in Early Modern England', in A L Beier, D Cannadine and J M Rosenheim (eds), op cit, p228; P Slack, *Poverty and Policy in Tudor and Stuart England* (London, 1988), pp65-66; D C Coleman, 'Labour in the English Economy in the 17th Century', in E M Carus-Wilson (ed), *Essays in Economic History*, vol 2 (London, 1962), pp300-304.
79 J Cooke, *Unum Necessarium: Or, The Poore Man's Case* (London, 1648), pp27-28, 43.
80 *Tyranipocrit* (Rotterdam, 1649), pp17, 24.
81 *Trades Destruction is England's Ruine* (London, 1659).

Henry Hallhead, writing against enclosures in 1650, regarded cloth workers as so poverty stricken that they had nothing to lay up for posterity and in years of high food prices or trade depression were pinched and starved:

And herein by the way the gatherers of the labours of the poor are like the taskmasters that exact more and more upon them. And when did you see any, out of their mean and mere labour, marry their children and provide for their posterity in a comfortable manner?[82]

One of the Diggers protested that labourers must 'go with cap in hand, and bended knee, to gentlemen and farmers, begging and entreating to work with them for 8d or 10d a day, which does give them occasion to tyrannise over poor people'.[83]

The belief that the producer owned his own labour passed from the 'middle sort' to the wage labourers:

Though we keep ourselves close to our hard labours, breaking our due and necessary rest which should refresh us, whereby our lives become a burden to us, and yet our careful and diligent labour will afford us no other than a distracted, languishing and miserable life. For how can it be otherwise, seeing we cannot enjoy the benefit of our labours ourselves, but for the maintenance of idle persons, slow bellies who reign and ride over the common people in every parish as gods and kings.[84]

Gerrard Winstanley, the Digger leader, perceived that the poor had their labour stolen from them. He visualised that the landless poor were a conquered people who had been dispossessed by their conquerors (the ruling class), who forced them to labour for wages and as 'slaves to work for them that had taken their property of their labours from them by the sword'. As a result, 'at this very day poor people are forced to work in some places for four, five, and six pence a day; in other places for eight, ten, and twelve pence a day, for such small prizes...that their earnings cannot find them bread for their family.' If they were reduced to homeless vagrants they were whipped, and if they stole to support themselves they were hanged.[85]

Throughout history there was a recurrent popular fantasy of a magical world of plenty which all enjoyed without having to work.[86] Similarly,

---

82   B Sharp, 'Common Rights, Charities, and the Disorderly Poor', op cit, p111.
83   G H Sabine (ed), op cit, pp656-657.
84   K Thomas, 'Another Digger Broadside', *Past and Present* 42 (1960), pp62-63.
85   G H Sabine (ed), op cit, p388.
86   A L Morton, *The English Utopia*, ch 1 (1952, reprinted London, 1978).

there was a dream that in the millennium, when Jesus Christ would establish his kingdom on earth, which in the 1640s and 1650s was thought to be imminent, the grinding toil of the labourer would cease. A Nottinghamshire girl, who was believed in 1641 to have returned from the dead, announced, 'The day of rest coming to rejoice us, our charge shall be taken away, and our travail shall have an end.' Some thought that work would cease altogether, but Mary Cary, a prominent millenarian, thought that men would still 'follow several employments, as now they do, but doubtless in a more regular and comfortable way... Some shall not labour and toil day and night...to maintain others that live viciously in idleness, drunkenness and other evil practices...[but] comfortably enjoy the work of their own hands.' Bernard Capp concludes:

> This perhaps was the nub of the popular vision. A world with no work
> at all was almost inconceivable except as an idle dream; but work freed
> from the burdens of rent, taxes, tithes, excise, and manorial dues was
> an image of earthly paradise with instant appeal.[87]

At the height of the revolution the Diggers campaigned for the abolition of wage labour. Their alternative was for the poor to regain possession of the main means of production in their society—the land. Their aim was to abolish rents and wages and to form communes in which the poor would cultivate the land collectively and share its produce according to their needs. This attracted some peasant smallholders who began to form such communities on common and waste lands (a radical alternative to enclosure into individual holdings for private gain), but the movement was crushed by force by landlords and richer farmers before it had time to grow to any size, though it may have had many hidden sympathisers among the poor.[88]

The increase in the number of full time wage workers and their degradation probably fostered among them an approach to consciousness of themselves as a distinct class, and created a potential for class conflict in those areas where capitalism was taking control. Alan Everitt says that on large farms where wage labourers were employed in producing for the market, the farmers' eyes became 'firmly fixed on prices and profits', and they 'ceased to think of their labourers as their own "folk" and neighbours' but 'as mere employees, to be taken on or dismissed at pleasure, as commercial prudence alone dictated'. In such a

---

87 B Cap, 'The Fifth Monarchists and Popular Millenarianism', in J F McGregor and
     B Reay (eds), *Radical Religion in the English Revolution* (Oxford, 1984), pp187-188.
88 K Thomas, op cit; J Gurney, 'Gerrard Winstanley and the Digger Movement in Walton
     and Cobham', *The Historical Journal*, vol 37 (1994); S Hindle, op cit, pp76-77.

situation 'the frictions between masters and men were often acute' and from the time of the civil war took on more of a relationship between 'antagonistic classes'.[89] In cloth making areas where some of the most militant support for parliament appeared in the civil war, J A Sharpe discerns amongst the wage workers 'a nascent class consciousness' and outbreaks of hostility towards 'their social superiors in general'.[90] Buchanan Sharp judges that in such areas there appeared 'sentiments approaching class hatred' and 'violent outbreaks of what can only be called class hatred for the wealthy'.[91]

At the same time the most visible signs of impoverishment were crowds of beggars in the streets and gangs of vagrants on the roads. Many of the poor migrated to London, where they hoped to find casual employment, but were often obliged to become beggars, thieves or prostitutes. In London, as in other large cities of pre-industrial Europe, unskilled casual labour accumulated, working as dockers, porters, road sweepers, water carriers and navvies. During the English Revolution they may have provided recruits for London 'mobs', but Christopher Hill regards them as 'basically non-political'.[92] Some of them died in the streets from hunger or exposure.[93]

Hill stresses the hostility towards wage labour in 17th century England, and the strategies evolved to evade or escape it. This may be regarded as an early manifestation of a proletarian ideology—one which was incompatible with capitalism—but as capitalism developed, wage earners initiated trade unions and industrial action which meant a de facto acceptance of wage work, and recognition that capitalism was an established system and the direction of the efforts of wage earners to improving their lot under it.[94]

Resistance to enclosures and to wage labour provide the background to the egalitarian ideas which will be examined in the next chapter, because the loss of common rights and the compulsion to work for wages were attributed to the power of the rich in an unequal society.

89   A Everitt, op cit, pp440-441, 464-465.
90   J A Sharpe, *Crime in 17th Century England* (Cambridge, 1983), pp18-19, 204, 208-209.
91   B Sharp, *In Contempt of all Authority*, op cit, pp8, 264.
92   F J Fisher, 'The Growth of London', in E W Ives (ed), *The English Revolution 1600-1660* (London, 1968), p78; J Merrington, op cit, pp187-188; C Hill, *The World Turned Upside Down* (London, 1972), pp33-34, 35-36; H Burstin, 'Unskilled Labour in Paris', in T M Safley and L N Rosenband (eds), op cit, pp63-64.
93   A L Beier, *Masterless Men...*, op cit, pp42, 46.
94   C Hill, 'Pottage for Freeborn Englishmen: Attitudes to Wage Labour', *Change and Continuity in 17th Century England* (London, 1974); C Hill, *Liberty Against the Law* (London, 1996).

Chapter 2

Equality

Trotsky's conception of 'dual power' or 'double sovereignty' was one of his most important contributions to the analysis of revolutions. The English Revolution was fought out in a series of armed struggles. The ancien regime broke down in 1640-42. Civil war meant that the royal government and the aristocracy were no longer in control. The aristocracy was split and there were two governments controlling different parts of the country—the king's government at Oxford and the parliament's government at Westminster. Victory for parliament created a new sort of duality, in that the New Model Army emerged as an independent centre of power in competition with the power of parliament. The army achieved dominance through a military *coup d'état* in 1648-49. As Trotsky said, 'The English Revolution of the 17th century…affords a clear example of this alternating dual power, with sharp transitions in the form of civil war'.[1] The struggle was for political power—for control of the state—and to re-establish unitary power in place of dual power: 'The development of a revolution lays bare at each stage the problem of power'.[2]

Revolution in England in the mid-17th century is defined by the overthrow of the monarchy, the House of Lords and the church. The political power of the old ruling class was eclipsed but a new ruling class did not clearly define itself and did not firmly seat itself in power, and there was a situation of dual power between the old ruling class and the new holders of power—army officers, republican politicians, elements amongst merchants of the City of London, and leaders of radical religious sects. The seizure of power by Oliver Cromwell imposed a temporary stability upon a highly unstable situation. After Cromwell's death in 1658 there was again competition for power between army

1   L Trotsky, *The History of the Russian Revolution*, translated by M Eastman (1932-33, reprinted London, 1977), pp223-231.
2   L Trotsky, op cit, p755.

and parliament, until stability was regained by the restoration of the monarchy in 1660.

'The immediate causes of the events of a revolution are changes in the state of mind of the conflicting classes', wrote Trotsky. 'Changes in the collective consciousness have naturally a semi-concealed character. Only when they have attained a certain degree of intensity do the new moods and ideas break to the surface.' Engels spoke of the struggles for power in a revolution working upon the minds of the participants and onlookers until they explode in new, political and religious ideas which influence the course of these struggles, 'and in many cases preponderate in determining their form', but still within assumptions created by the economic conditions of the different social groups.[3] The writers, speakers and leaders at all levels who were thrown up by these struggles reflected and expressed in varying degrees the interests of social groups and classes.

Peter Laslett tries to establish that 17th century England was a 'one class society'. His objective is to eliminate class conflict, but his one class is the ruling class, and by accepting and confirming that there is a ruling class he demonstrates that England was a class society.[4] Morrill and Walter argue that in mid-17th century England the danger of a popular social revolution was an illusion in the minds of nobility and gentry, but in so doing they confirm the class consciousness of the ruling class and its sense of being engaged in class struggle, and that formed its attitudes and actions before and during the revolution.[5] The very fact of the existence of propaganda to persuade the people to accept the existing distribution of wealth and the existing structure of authority, and the very fact of the existence of concern to hold down the masses, and to prevent or crush popular revolts are evidence of the existence of a class society: class struggle is waged from the top down as well as from the bottom up.[6]

Shifting relations of the class of small producers, on the one hand with the aristocracy and on the other hand with the labouring poor, were causes of the outbreak, course and outcome of the revolution. In a bourgeois revolution there are two possible pathways—the one seeking

3   L Trotsky, op cit, p755; Letter from Frederick Engels to J Bloch (1890), in K Marx and F Engels, *Selected Works*, vol II (2 vols, Moscow, 1649-50), p443.
4   P Laslett, *The World We Have Lost* (London, third edition, 1983), ch 2.
5   J Morrill and J Walter, 'Order and Disorder in the English Revolution', in A Fletcher and J Stevenson (eds), *Order and Disorder in Early Modern England* (Cambridge, 1985), pp147, 149-150, 164-165.
6   G E M de Ste Croix, *The Class Struggle in the Ancient Greek World* (London, third impression, 1997), pp65-66.

change through compromise with the old ruling order (monarchy and aristocracy) and the other seeking change through the overthrow of the monarchy and the aristocracy.[7] In the end the first of those tendencies triumphed in the English Revolution. The permanent overthrow of the monarchy and the aristocracy did not take place, and it would have required a greater degree of popular pressure than occurred. It is a mistake to separate political revolution from social revolution, for the 'political revolution' of 1648-49 was rooted in social forces, but the question is whether the seizure of power in 1648-49 might have moved on to the destruction of the existing economic and social order. Since the labouring poor had the least interest in the existing economic and social order, such an extension and intensification of the revolution would have had to be based on them. This is the subject of this chapter and its focus is upon what I call 'the far left' in the English Revolution—those who sought to speak for and mobilise the labouring poor.

Religion and the poor

The trial and execution of the king, the abolition of the monarchy and the House of Lords, and the establishment of a republic in 1649 led some to hope for and expect further extension of the revolution—the abolition of tithes (the tax for support of the clergy of the established church) and of a state church, the decentralisation of the legal system and the erection of local courts staffed by juries of neighbours, without professional judges or lawyers. But further than that there was the possibility of the revolution being extended by plebeian elements below the level of the 'middling sort' to attacks on the existing social and economic order.[8] The latter tendency embraced the groups called 'Diggers' by their opponents, individuals scandalised as 'Ranters' by their critics, and also elements of the Levellers, Fifth Monarchists and Quakers. This tendency was characterised by class feeling, dreams of equality, schemes for the decentralisation of power, 'practical christianity', and hopes for the redistribution of wealth. It foreshadows socialism.

Many historians believe that in early modern England there was a dominant culture which had the capacity to absorb and contain subversion, and that a thoroughgoing revolution could take place only if that dominant culture was rejected root and branch. But this culture

7   A Klíma, 'The Bourgeois Revolution of 1848-9 in Central Europe', in R Porter and
      M Teich (eds), Revolution in History (Cambridge, 1986), pp76, 79-80, 97-98.
8   C Hill, The World Turned Upside Down: Radical Ideas during the English Revolution
      (London, 1972), pp12-13, 275.

of the ruling class was reinterpreted and modified in the course of its assimilation by the lower classes. This was facilitated by the fact the culture common to both upper and lower classes was a biblical culture, which could be interpreted in two ways—to defend the existing order or to attack the existing order. It contained within it subversive possibilities when transmitted through the experiences and traditions of the poor, and presented the potential for carrying the revolution to more extreme social changes. Similarly, the law did not merely make the people submissive to the ruling class, but it was subject to different interpretations by the elite and the masses, and the people had their own concepts of legality which were not the same as those of their masters.[9]

The main component of the dominant culture was Christianity, or rather Protestant Christianity, as interpreted by the old aristocratic ruling class or, rather differently, by the emerging bourgeoisie. But there is a question of how far the plebeian masses were influenced by the established Church of England. Keith Thomas provides evidence that many of the poor were ignorant of the basics of Christianity, did not attend church regularly and behaved irreverently when they did. It was said that they preferred tales about Robin Hood to sermons, and knew more of those tales than they did of bible stories.[10] Alehouses functioned as centres of popular irreligion, where many of the poor occupied themselves with drink and games on Sundays instead of going to church.[11] But Margaret Spufford points to the involvement of the 'poorer sort' and the 'humblest of the laity' in debates on religion. She accepts that some parishioners were hostile to religion, others were deeply committed, and the rest apathetic, though it cannot be said what proportion fell into each category.[12] During the revolutionary years some of the London populace engaged in heated debates in shops and alehouses about religion, and even in the streets, including the raising of questions about the fundamentals of faith. In a Southwark

9   G Rudé, *Ideology and Popular Protest* (London, 1980), p36; R H Hilton, *Class Conflict and the Crisis of Feudalism* (London, revised second edition, 1990); P Burke, 'Revolution and Popular Culture', in R Porter and M Teich (eds), op cit, pp209, 213; A Woods, 'Custom, Identity and Resistance: English Free Miners and their Law c1550-1800', in P Griffiths, A Fox and S Hindle (eds), *The Experience of Authority in Early Modern England* (London, 1996), pp278-279.

10 K Thomas, *Religion and the Decline of Magic: Studies in Popular Beliefs in 16th and 17th Century England* (Harmondsworth, 1973), pp189-195.

11 P Clark, *The English Alehouse: A Social History 1200-1830* (London, 1983), pp154, 157-158.

12 M Spufford, 'Puritanism and Social Control?' in A Fletcher and J Stevenson (eds), op cit, pp44-46, and *Small Books and Pleasant Histories: Popular Fiction and its Readership in 17th Century England* (London, 1981), pp194-196.

shop a hatmaker, a cordwainer and a joiner debated Socinianism (denial of the divinity of Christ). In a Lambeth alehouse three illiterate watermen argued how salvation was to be achieved.[13] Richard Baxter in his ministry at Kidderminster in the 1650s found that 'some of the poor men did competently understand the body of divinity, and were able to judge in difficult controversies: some of them were so able in prayer that few ministers did match them in order and fullness, and apt expressions, and holy oratory, with fervency; abundance of them were able to pray very laudably with their families, or with others.' When he preached at Dudley in Worcestershire 'the poor nailers and other labourers would not only crowd the church as full as ever I saw any in London, but also hang upon the windows and the leads without'.[14]

Generally there was popular involvement with the church and its services in relation to the rites of passage—baptism, marriage, burial. Martin Ingram has no doubt that 'the christianity which officially dominated Tudor and Stuart society was in some sense accepted by the mass of the people'. But in what sense, for he adds that 'precisely what the religious beliefs of ordinary people amounted to is a moot point'? The same symbols, rituals and texts may be understood in different ways, and 'ordinary lay people' may experience and understand 'certain aspects of faith and practice differently from their clerical masters'.[15] Further than that, the religious ideas and teachings of the elite, notably the local squire and the minister of the parish, may have been translated and absorbed by the poor into terms more meaningful to their own traditions, experiences, and needs.[16] This was compatible with conformity to the rites of the established church, and that seems to have been the case with most people, but a distinctive feature of the revolutionary period was the emergence of groups that gave public expression to radical reinterpretation of religion to give overt expression of resistance to the ruling class.

Engels put it well when he discerned that the domination of religion in the medieval and early modern periods meant that the poor could put forward their own interests only through religion. 'Each of the different classes uses its own appropriate religion,' he said. He interpreted

---

13 K Lindley, *Popular Politics and Religion in Civil War London* (Aldershot, 1997), p289.
14 M Sylvester (ed), *Relquiae Baxterianae* (London, 1986), p85.
15 M Ingram, 'From Reformation to Toleration: Popular Religious Culture in England, 1540-1690', in T Harris (ed), *Popular Culture in England, c1500-1850* (London, 1995), pp96, 108-109, 110; A W Smith, 'Popular Religion', *Past and Present* 40 (1968), pp181-186.
16 B Reay, 'Popular Religion', in B Reay (ed), *Popular Culture in 17th Century England* (London, 1988), p98.

religious beliefs in terms of 'class relations', and suggested that the propertyless plebeians and labourers, 'precursors of the later proletariat', developed a plebeian version of christianity.[17] But when he said that 'the class struggles of that day were clothed in religious shibboleths', and 'the interests, requirements, and demands of the various classes were concealed behind a religious screen', his language missed the close integration of class interests and class struggles with religious language and religious beliefs.

Christopher Hill demonstrates that when the Protestant Reformation led to the translating and printing of the Bible in English it provided a source for denunciation of the rich and powerful, and for ideas of social justice and ending exploitation and arbitrary power. 'Go to now, ye rich men; weep and howl for your miseries that shall come upon you' (James). God 'will bring down them that dwell on high', promised Isaiah: 'the feet of the poor...shall tread [them] down.' 'They shall not build, and another inhabit; they shall not plant, and another eat.' The phrase 'turning the world upside down', which was much quoted during the English Revolution, was taken from Isaiah and Acts. Denunciation of oppression was expressed in the Old Testament's celebration of liberation from Egyptian taskmasters and from captivity in Babylon.[18] That this was part of popular culture is evidenced by the way in which biblical references continued to be used by the labouring poor until well into the 19th century: 'class hostility was enunciated in biblical language'.[19]

The Marxist conception of an economic base and an ideological superstructure may slip into, or be misinterpreted as, a crude economic determinism, but this is due to omitting the crucial intervening factor of class relations, which are formed by economic conditions but which give rise to ideology via the medium of class consciousness and class struggle. The religion of the far left revolutionaries in the late 1640s and early 1650s was a statement of class differences and was motivated by class struggle.

17 F Engels, 'Ludwig Feuerbach and the End of Classical German Philosophy', in K Marx and F Engels, *Selected Works*, op cit, vol II, pp361-362, and F Engels, *The Peasant War in Germany* (Moscow, 1965), pp41-42.

18 C Hill, *The English Bible and the Seventeenth-Century Revolution* (London, 1993), pp155-164.

19 K D M Snell, 'Deferential Bitterness: The Social Outlook of the Rural Proletariat in 18th and 19th Century England and Wales', in M L Bush (ed), *Social Order and Social Classes in Europe since 1500: Studies in Social Stratification* (London, 1992), pp171-176.

The search for equality

Concern for the poor, for the deprived, for the handicapped, for the sick and the old, for the oppressed and the persecuted, is the seedbed of socialism. Condemnation of the economic and social gulf between rich and poor, and of the consequences of inequality, was the motivating force for the far left revolutionaries. Gerrard Winstanley, the Digger leader, observed that a few men had vast estates in land but most men had little or no land, 'and thereby some are lifted up into the chair of tyranny, and others trod under the footstool of misery, as if the earth was made for a few, not for all men'.[20] A Quaker addressed 'lords, ladies, knights, gentlemen, and gentlewomen' that 'because of your much earth, which by fraud, deceit, and oppression you have gotten together, you are exalted above your fellow creatures, and grind the faces of the poor, and they are as slaves under you, and must labour and toil under you, and you must live at ease'.[21] George Foster reproached the wealthy that because of their riches they 'have thought themselves better than others, and must have your fellow creatures in bondage to you, and they must serve you, as work for you, and moil and toil for you, and stand cap in hand to you, and must not displease you, no by no means'.[22] The poorly paid labourers who tilled their lands were esteemed by the rich less than their dogs and horses. Indeed, the upper classes regarded the poor as subhuman, semi-animal: they were 'beastlike', 'the vile and brutish part of mankind', their occupations were 'bestial' because their function was to toil like beasts of burden in the service of their masters.[23] The anonymous author of *Tyranipocrit* denounced the parasitism and complacency of the well to do:

> As for some to have so many hundred pounds a year for doing nothing, or for executing of some needless office, or to oversee and command others, etc and a poor labouring man must work for three or four pence a day, and we uncharitable partial wretches can behold all this and be silent, and we pass it over as a matter not worthy of our considerations.[24]

William Walwyn, one of the leaders of the Levellers, who tended towards the far left, challenged the rich:

20 G H Sabine (ed), *The Works of Gerrard Winstanley* (1941, reprinted New York, 1965), pp158-159.
21 Quoted by B Reay, *The Quakers and the English Revolution* (New York, 1985), p39.
22 Quoted by A L Morton, *The World of the Ranters: Religious Radicalism in the English Revolution* (London, 1970), p87.
23 K Thomas, *Man and the Natural World* (London, 1984), pp41-47.
24 *Tyranipocrit* (Rotterdam, 1649), pp17, 24.

Look about you and you will find…thousands of miserable, distressed, starved…Christians: see how pale and wan they look; how coldly, raggedly, and unwholesomely they are clothed; live one week with them in their poor houses, lodge as they lodge, eat as they eat, and no oftener, and be at the same pass to get that wretched food for a sickly wife, and hunger-starved children; (if you dare do this for fear of death or diseases).

Then walk abroad and see men and women 'abounding in all things that can be imagined', and having 'more than suffices', as 'their silks, their beavers [fur hats], their rings' testify.[25] The rich 'do spend more in one day than a poor man has to spend in a year', they ride by in coaches drawn by six horses while the poor have no shoes, and 'old, lame, blind, and impotent persons [ie physically weak], must crawl on the way'.[26]

How had this come about? By force and fraud, said these pamphleteers, the people had had the land stolen from them and had been compelled to work for these 'robbers', who were made rich by the labours of the poor. The wealthy took and monopolised political power and dominated the state, which protected their riches.[27]

Dreams of equality form the socialist spirit, and in the 17th century we are talking literally of dreams, for Gerrard Winstanley the Digger and Abiezer Coppe the Ranter both received their messages directly from god in dreams.[28] The poor resented not only their poverty but also being despised for it. Sometimes their response was to imagine a reversal of roles—the world turned upside down, which was an imagery imprinted in the popular mind of early modern Europe.[29] Coppe's vision was that 'kings, princes, lords, great ones, must bow to the poorest peasants; rich men must stoop to poor rogues'.[30] But the aim was equality. *Tyranipocrit* dreamed of a world in which the king and the beggar, the queen and the kitchen maid would be equal.[31] 'Every one shall look upon each other as equal in the creation', proclaimed Winstanley.[32] Coppe very specifically extended equality to 'the poorest

25 J R McMichael and B Taft (eds), *The Writings of William Walwyn* (Athens, Georgia, 1989), p80.
26 *Tyranipocrit*, op cit, pp30, 50, 51.
27 G H Sabine (ed), op cit, pp179, 190; *Tyranipocrit*, op cit, pp27-28, 33, 49, 50; B Reay, *The Quakers…*, op cit, pp39-40.
28 G H Sabine (ed), op cit, pp190, 261-262; N Smith (ed), *A Collection of Ranter Writings from the 17th Century* (London, 1983), pp82-83, 99.
29 P Burke, *Popular Culture in Early Modern Europe* (London, 1978), pp188-190, 203-205; A L Morton, *The English Utopia*, ch I (1952, reprinted London, 1969).
30 N Smith (ed), op cit, p109.
31 *Tyranipocrit*, op cit, p52.
32 G H Sabine (ed), op cit, p159.

and most depressed strata of society', 'the most wretched and submerged elements of the population'.[33]

> Each beggar that you meet
> Fall down before him, kiss him in the street.

> He is thy brother, thy fellow, flesh of thy flesh.

> Turn not away thine eyes from thine own FLESH... Mine ears are filled brim full with cries of poor prisoners, Newgate, Ludgate cries...are seldom out of mine ears. Those doleful cries, Bread, bread, bread for the Lord's sake, pierce mine ears and heart, I can no longer forbear. Wherefore hie you apace to all prisons in the kingdom, bow before those poor, nasty, lousy, ragged wretches, say to them, your humble servants, sirs...we let you go free, and serve you.

(Poor prisoners had to depend on charity for subsistence: 'Newgate' and 'Ludgate' were prisons.) Cripples, beggars, rogues, thieves, gypsies, said Coppe, are 'mine own brethren and sisters, flesh of my flesh, and as good as the greatest lord in England'.[34] *Tyranipocrit's* compassion extended to 'the poor Irish' and to slaves in English colonies.[35] But equality of status must be based on equality of wealth, in which, as Winstanley said, all would have sufficient to live comfortably.[36] A true reformation 'would give unto every man like means to live on', wrote *Tyranipocrit*, and would give all children 'like education', and would maintain and cherish all old, weak, and impotent persons.[37]

Demands for equality were age old in Europe and burst forth again in the French Revolution.[38] They found their authority in the Christian doctrine of the 'equality of the children of god' and from the practice of the early Christians.[39] Quakers in the English Revolution insisted on 'equality in all things, man with man', because mankind was 'made of one blood and mould, being the sons of Adam by nature, and all children of god by creation.[40] Peasant appeals to 'custom' to defend themselves against increases of exploitation by feudal lords involved the acceptance of the existing structure of society. But invoking religious

33 A L Morton, *The World of the Ranters...*, op cit, pp71, 87.
34 N Smith (ed), op cit, pp90-91, 105.
35 *Tyranipocrit*, op cit, pp23, 35.
36 G H Sabine (ed), op cit, pp179-180.
37 *Tyranipocrit*, op cit, pp4, 19, 20, 51-52.
38 A Soboul, *The Parisian Sans-Culottes and the French Revolution*, translated by G Lewis (Oxford, 1964), ch II.
39 F Engels, *The Peasant War in Germany*, op cit, pp44-45.
40 W Schenk, *The Concern for Social Justice in the Puritan Revolution* (London, 1948), pp122-123.

sanction for equality was revolutionary because it allowed for the overthrow of the existing economic and social order and its replacement by a wholly different one based on Christian equality.[41] The slogan of the English peasant revolt of the 14th century—'When Adam delved and Eve span, who was then the gentleman?'—continued to echo down the centuries and was much quoted in the 1640s. John Ball probably did say, 'For what reason do they hold us in bondage? Are we not all descended from the same parents Adam and Eve? And what can they show or what reason can they give why they should be more masters than ourselves?' Rodney Hilton sees these ideas reflected in Colonel Rainborough's famous statement in 1647 at the debates in the army on a new constitution for England, defending an extension of the franchise for parliamentary elections: 'The poorest he that is in England hath a life to live as the greatest he.' Hilton calls this 'an expression of an English tradition as ancient as the more publicised traditions of reverence for old-established institutions'.[42]

The form of appeal to religion pre-eminent amongst the revolutionaries in the English Revolution was of a war against Antichrist, in which success would usher in the rule of Christ. Parliamentarians saw the civil war as a fight between Christ and Antichrist. Winstanley extended this from a struggle against Antichristian bishops and royalists to a struggle against the whole ruling class:[43]

> For such a government as preserves part and destroys another part of creation is not the power of Christ but of Antichrist; that government that gives liberty to the gentry to have all the earth, and shut out the poor commoners from enjoying any part, ruling by the tyrannical law of conquest over brethren, this is the government of imaginary, self-seeking Antichrist; and every plant which our heavenly father hath not planted, shall be rooted out.

He believed that the 'Antichristian captivity' of the people was about to end in 1649.[44] The poor of Sutton in the Isle of Ely saw their struggle against the loss of their common rights in the fens as part of a general conflict between rich and poor. They said that they had 'found by woeful experience the proverb to be true, wealth makes

41 B Scribner and G Benecke (eds), *The German Peasant War of 1525—New Viewpoints* (London, 1979), pp12, 19-21, 41, 43, 48-50.
42 R H Hilton, op cit, pp10, 65; C Hill, *Milton and the Puritan Revolution* (1977, reprinted London, 1997), pp71-72.
43 C Hill, *Antichrist in 17th Century England* (London, 1971), ch III.
44 G H Sabine (ed), op cit, pp230, 472.

many friends, but the poor is separate from his neighbour' (Proverbs: 19.4). They awaited in 1649 the day 'when in this nation the poor do enjoy their own'.[45]

Decentralisation of power

There are two messages from the Levellers and the Diggers that have echoed down the generations. One is that power corrupts and leaders betray, and the other is that meaningful popular participation and control are possible only by the decentralisation of power to smaller units.

'When public officers remain long in place of judicature, they will degenerate from the bounds of humility, honesty and tender care of brethren', wrote Winstanley, 'in regard the heart of man is so subject to be overspread with the clouds of covetousness, pride and vainglory; for though at the first entrance into places of rule they be of public spirits, seeking the freedom of others as their own, yet continuing long in such a place, where honour and greatness is coming in, they become selfish, seeking themselves, and not common freedom, as experience proves it true in these days'.[46] The Leveller leaders learnt 'by woeful experience…the prevalence of corrupt interests powerfully inclining most men once entrusted with authority to pervert the same to their own domination, and to the prejudice of our peace and liberties':

> We confess indeed, that the experimental defections of so many men as have succeeded in authority, and the exceeding difference we have hitherto found in the same men in a low and in an exalted condition, make us even mistrust our own hearts, and hardly to believe our own resolution to the contrary. And therefore we have proposed such an establishment, as supposing men to be too flexible and yielding to worldly temptations, they should not yet have a means or opportunity either to injure particulars, or prejudice the public, without extreme hazard and apparent danger to themselves.[47]

For both Levellers and Diggers the solution was decentralisation, which 'was the indispensable condition for the democratisation of the whole political system in church and state', and devolution of power to local communities.[48]

---

45   K Lindley, op cit, pp142-143.
46   G H Sabine (ed), op cit, p540.
47   D M Wolfe (ed), *Leveller Manifestoes of the Puritan Revolution* (1944, reprinted London, 1967), pp394, 405.
48   F D Dow, *Radicalism in the English Revolution 1640-1660* (Oxford, 1985), pp43, 78.

Winstanley's underlying conception of the future society was, in some ways, similar to that of the Levellers, especially as laid down in their manifesto of May 1649: the centre of gravity was to lie in the small local community.[49]

The officers of local government were to be elected annually, according to both the Levellers' *Agreement of the People* of May 1649 and Winstanley's *Law of Freedom* (1651), by an electorate consisting of 'all men of the age of one and twenty years and upwards (not being servants or receiving alms...', in the Levellers' formula, and 'all men from 20 years of age upwards', in Winstanley's less restrictive formula, but he excluded those under 40 years of age from being elected save in exceptional circumstances.[50] The church would fall under local control, the Levellers demanding that ministers should no longer be imposed on parishes but the parishioners be given 'free liberty...to choose such as themselves shall approve, and upon such terms and for such rewards as themselves shall be willing to contribute or shall contract for'.[51] Under Winstanley's scheme the people of a parish would choose a minister to serve for a year, but his functions would be far more secular than the Levellers visualised. He would communicate news, read out the laws of the commonwealth, and institute discussions of history, arts and sciences, and 'the nature of mankind':

> He who is the chosen minister for that year to read, shall not be the only man to make sermons or speeches, but everyone who has any experience, and is able to speak of any art or language, or of the nature of the heavens above or of the earth below, shall have free liberty to speak... Yet he who is the reader may have his liberty to speak too, but not to assume all the power to himself, as the proud and ignorant clergy have done.[52]

Both Levellers and Winstanley sought to reduce central control over the legal system and to institutionalise the traditional, informal justice exercised within the local community. The *Agreement of the People* insisted that there should be no other way of judgement, 'or conviction of life, limb, liberty, or estate, but only by 12 sworn men of the neighbourhood, to be chosen in some free way by the people'.[53]

---

49 W Schenk, op cit, pp105-106.
50 D M Wolfe (ed), op cit, pp402-403, G H Sabine (ed), op cit, pp540-541, 543-544, 545-546, 596.
51 D M Wolfe (ed), op cit, p408.
52 G H Sabine (ed), op cit, pp562-565.
53 D M Wolfe (ed), op cit, pp407-408.

Winstanley visualised elected 'peacemakers' in every parish or town to reconcile differences between individuals and to deal with minor offenders, and county courts, composed of a judge and representatives of the local communities, to deal with more serious offences.[54]

Both Levellers and Winstanley were concerned with the control of military power. 'And forasmuch as nothing threatens greater danger to the commonwealth than that the military power should by any means come to be superior to the civil authority', the Levellers argued that there should be no standing army. When a military force had to be raised, it could be done only by parliament, which would allot to each county, city, town and borough, a quota of the men to be enlisted, but the electorate would choose the officers of the regiments, troops and companies, and remove them if they saw cause, except that the commander in chief of the army and the general staff would be appointed by parliament.[55] Winstanley provided that in peacetime there would be soldiers under the command of the officers of local government, but in the event of invasion from abroad or insurrection at home, parliament would raise and direct an army.[56]

However, there would be a great difference between the structure of the communities to which the Levellers and Winstanley would devolve power, because under the former production would be in private hands and the existing distribution of wealth would be unchanged, while under the latter there would be the elimination of differences of wealth and a communal system of production.

'Practical Christianity'

The far left revolutionaries operated within a Christian and Protestant ideology, but one which did not arise wholly from the ruling class, or from the professional clergy, or from the 'middle sort of people', but was shaped by the experiences and needs of the poor. They found the essence of religion not in theology, sacraments, ceremonies and rituals of the church, but in what they termed 'practical Christianity', or one might say 'social Christianity'. It may be identified with good neighbourliness.[57]

54   G H Sabine (ed), op cit, pp544-548, 554-556.
55   D M Wolfe (ed), op cit, p409.
56   G H Sabine (ed), op cit, pp552-553, 561-562, 571-576.
57   B Manning, 'The Levellers and Religion', in J F McGregor and B Reay (eds), *Radical Religion in the English Revolution* (Oxford, 1984), pp68-78; J C Davis, 'The Levellers and Christianity', in B Manning (ed), *Politics, Religion and the English Civil War* (London, 1973), pp234-236; W Schenk, op cit, pp47-49; M Weber, *The Sociology of Religion* (Boston, 1963), pp211-212.

Walwyn exemplified this and defined a 'pure and undefiled religion' as one which resulted 'in feeding the hungry, clothing the naked, visiting and comforting the sick, relieving the aged, weak and impotent', and 'in freeing a commonwealth from all tyrants, oppressors, and deceivers'. He reproached the so called 'religious people' who were 'not so hasty to run into his poor neighbour's house to see what is wanting there, he may lie upon a bed or no bed, covering or no covering, be starved through cold and hunger, overburdened with labour, be sick, lame or diseased', but these things do not trouble them.[58] This was echoed by Winstanley, who identified true religion with 'feeding the hungry, clothing the naked, relieving the oppressed'.[59] Peter Chamberlen, a physician and Fifth Monarchist, maintained that it was 'the work of nature, reason and Christianity, by which we shall be judged in the last day (Matthew: 25), and the very bottom of all pretences in all states, councils, and corporations: "To clothe the naked, feed the hungry, visit the sick, and relieve the oppressed".'[60] Christopher Chisman (or Cheeseman), a Leveller soldier and later a Quaker, placed 'practical Christianity' in the context of class conflict:

> The religion of the great ones of our age is a mere shadow, and all their pulpit-prattling is nothing; they are only wolves in sheep's clothing; they are devils transformed into angels of light. But pure religion and undefiled, is to visit the fatherless and widows, and to keep ourselves unspotted in the world, which the great professors of our time will not do I am sure; for they add house to house, land to land, nay thousands to ten thousands, while the poor of the kingdom are ready to starve.[61]

Coppe repeated a sentiment that was also much quoted by Walwyn:

> He that has this world's goods and sees his brother in want, and shuts up the bowels of compassion from him, the love of god dwells not in him, this man's religion is in vain. His religion is in vain that sees his brother in want, etc. His brother—a beggar, a lazar [a poor and diseased person], a cripple, yea a cutpurse, a thief in the gaol, etc. He that sees such a brother, flesh of his flesh, in want, and shuts up the bowels of his compassion from him, the love of god dwells not in him, his religion is in vain.[62]

58 J R McMichael and B Taft (eds), op cit, pp80, 269, 324, 329-330.
59 G H Sabine (ed), op cit, pp111, 193.
60 P Chamberlen, *The Poore Mans Advocate* (London, 1649), p47.
61 C Chisman, *The Lamb Contending with the Lion* (1649).
62 N Smith (ed), op cit, p115.

On the basis of 'practical Christianity' J C Davis links Coppe with Walwyn and Winstanley and George Foster.[63] *Tyranipocrit* turned away from the doctrine that lay at the heart of Protestantism—justification by faith alone—because it could not help the poor. Faith, he said, was not 'absolutely necessary to salvation'. What was absolutely necessary was 'the love of god, in Christ…[which is] to love your neighbour as yourself… Now to love our neighbours as ourselves, the rule is always in us, we need not…go to church, nor hear preachers, nor read books, to attain to this knowledge'.[64]

Redistribution of wealth

'Practical Christianity' leads to more than a conventional call for the well to do to be more charitable to the poor because it opens up the question of redistribution of wealth. Walwyn said that 'practical Christianity' would 'empty the fullest bags and pluck down the highest plumes'.[65] For Winstanley it meant that the land must no longer be monopolised by 'a few to live at ease upon' but be made available 'for all to live comfortably upon'.[66] So it can hardly be dismissed as 'a vague and pragmatic concept', in Davis's judgement, lacking definition of the means to achieve its objectives.[67] It leads very concretely and precisely to the implementation of its ethics by demanding the expropriation of the rich and the redistribution of wealth to the poor—a fundamental principle of socialism.

The abiding popularity of tales of Robin Hood articulated the popular belief in the legitimacy of taking from the rich to give to the poor. In the two generations before the revolution, ballads about Robin Hood were widely popular and ten ballads on Robin Hood were registered in 1656-57.[68] Even Margaret Spufford has to agree that he was 'a folk hero' and that 'there was no doubt where his social sympathies lay':

Poor men might safely pass by him,
and some that way would choose,

63 J C Davis, *Fear, Myth and History: The Ranters and the Historians* (Cambridge, 1986), pp49-57; 'Fear, Myth and Furore: Reappraising the "Ranters",' *Past and Present*, 129 (1990), p101.
64 *Tyranipocrit*, op cit, pp20-21, 25, 35, 36.
65 J R McMichael and B Taft (eds), op cit, p269.
66 G H Sabine (ed), op cit, p193.
67 J C Davis, 'The Levellers and Christianity', op cit, p236.
68 C Hill, *Liberty Against the Law* (London, 1996), ch 5; E J Hobsbawm, *Bandits* (Harmondsworth, 1972).

for well they knew that to help them
he evermore did use.
But when he knew a miser rich
that did the poor oppress,
to feel his coin his hands did itch,
he'd have it, more or less.[69]

A strong motive was revenge for the oppressions and humiliations
the rich inflicted on the poor. This was a notable theme of the Fifth
Monarchists. Morgan Llwyd expected 'plague, flame, sword, and hail-
stones great' to fall upon the proud and mighty. Anna Trapnel looked
for god to 'batter' the great men of the world, and Thomas Venner
thought that his mission was to 'thrash the mountains' (an image for
the rich and powerful).[70] Shortly before he launched the Digger communes, Winstanley declared:

> And surely as the Scriptures threaten misery to rich men, bidding them
> 'Howl and weep, for their gold and silver is cankered, and the rust thereof
> cries unto heaven for vengeance against them'... Surely all those threat-
> enings shall be materially fulfilled, for they should be turned out of all,
> and their riches given to a people that will bring forth better fruit, and
> such as they have oppressed shall inherit the land. The rich man tells
> the poor, that they offend reason's law, if they take from the rich. I am
> sure it is a breach in that law in the rich to have plenty by them, and
> yet will see their fellow creatures, men and women, to starve for want.[71]

Coppe's message was the same as Winstanley's: 'The echoes of Winstanley', observes Davis, 'are particularly strong in Coppe':[72]

> Behold, behold, behold, I the eternal god, the lord of hosts, who am that
> mighty Leveller, am coming (yea even at the doors) to level in good
> earnest, to level to some purpose, to level with a witness, to level the hills
> with the valleys, and to lay the mountains low... For the lofty looks of man
> shall be humbled, and the haughtiness of men shall be bowed down.
>
> For lo I come (says the Lord) with a vengeance, to level also...your
> honour, pomp, greatness, superfluity, and confound it into parity, equal-
> ity, community; that the neck of horrid pride, murder, malice, and
> tyranny, etc may be chopped off at one blow.[73]

---

69   M Spufford, *Small Books and Pleasant Histories*, op cit, pp231-232.
70   B Capp, *The Fifth Monarchy Men: A Study in 17th Century English Millenarianism*
     (London, 1972), pp142-143.
71   G H Sabine (ed), op cit, pp181-182.
72   J C Davis, *Fear, Myth and History*, op cit, p54.
73   N Smith (ed), op cit, pp87, 88-89.

'I pass this sentence on you, O rich men', declared George Foster, 'that I will utterly destroy you', and the poor will be released from slavery and bondage to the rich. This would be not only in England but throughout the world: it would be an international revolution. Foster in 1650 had a vision of a man on a white horse 'cutting down all men and women that he met with that were higher than the middle sort, and raised up that were lower than the middle sort, and made them all equal; and cried out, "Equality, equality, equality"… I, the Lord of Hosts have done this… I will…make the low and poor equal with the rich'. God 'will make those that have riches give them to them that have none'. God, 'that mighty Leveller', will root up all powers, whether kings or parliaments and will make all common: the whole earth shall be a treasure for all and not for some. 'And if any say, "Why do they take away my goods?",' the answer will be because 'we have need of them, and we, in the name of our Creator, take them for to make use of them… And what will you say to this, O you great men that have abundance?'[74] As Christopher Hill aptly comments: 'This was not the god of the propertied classes'.[75]

Hill pointed out that Foster does not fit neatly into the category of Leveller or Ranter, and there are verbal echoes of Winstanley in his tracts. This is a good reason for avoiding the historian's desire to package the radicals into separate boxes, which conceals the fluidity of groupings in the revolutionary maelstrom. Common concerns and shared policies across the broad spectrum of radicalism need to be stressed. The Diggers cannot be so easily dismissed as peripheral or insignificant, or the Ranters treated as mere figments in the minds of the authorities, or Coppe and Foster regarded as isolated individuals, when they are all placed in the context of a far left tendency in the revolution and the principles for which they all fought.

'The inheritances of the rich shall be given to those poor, and there shall be no beggar in Israel', announced Winstanley. 'And there is equity and reason in it, for the King of Righteousness did not make some men to be tyrants, and others to be slaves, at the beginning'.[76] The far left revolutionaries regularly asserted that inequality of wealth was not from the beginning and was contrary to god's intentions when he created the world: their aim was to turn the world the right way up. They also invoked the example of the communism of the early Christians,

---

74   C Hill, *The World Turned Upside Down*, op cit, pp179-180.
75   C Hill, 'Plebeian Irreligion in 17th Century England', in C Hill, *England's Turning Point: Essays in 17th Century English History* (London, 1998), pp83-84.
76   G H Sabine (ed), op cit, pp181-182, 270.

who 'had all things common'.[77] Norman Cohn notes that 'the one thoroughly revolutionary social doctrine of the Middle Ages' was 'that human beings had at first lived as a community of equals holding all things in common and knowing nothing of "mine" and "thine".'[78]

There were, however, two methods proposed for the redistribution of wealth: one was to abolish private property and have all things in common, as the Diggers intended in the long run, and the other was to retain private property but to equalise all holdings. A pamphlet of 1654 wished:

> To redeem again the vineyard of the poor, which the Ahabs of the earth have taken away; to take away an house from them that have many, and a field from them who have plenty of more, to appoint for a portion to supply them that have none, until…he that has most, has nothing too much, and he that has least, have nothing lacking, that so…the land may grow up towards her true Sabbath, where she shall no more bring forth her children to oppression and bondage.[79]

The 'golden rule' of religion—'to do unto all man as we would have them to do unto us'—was much invoked by the radical revolutionaries.[80] From this *Tyranipocrit* drew the conclusion:

> Now what can be more just than to give to every man with discretion, that which god and nature has allotted them…it is all the goods that the rich persons have more than their poor neighbours, and that an equality of goods and lands might be made and maintained, so that no man might have more than his neighbour.

He devised a scheme by which everything above £100 a year would be confiscated and redistributed to those who had less than £100 a year.[81]

Of course there is a difference between, on the one hand, abolishing private property and introducing common ownership and, on the other hand, maintaining private property but equalising incomes.

77 J R McMichael and B Taft (eds), op cit, p80; *Tyranipocrit*, op cit, p19; *A Justification of the Mad Crew* (1650), reprinted in J C Davis, *Fear, Myth and History*, op cit, Appendix, p148.

78 N Cohn, 'Medieval Millenarianism', in S Thrupp (ed), *Millennial Dreams in Action* (New York, 1970), p37.

79 Quoted by P Zagorin, *A History of Political Thought in the English Revolution* (1954, reprinted Bristol, 1997), p101.

80 B Manning, 'The Levellers and Religion', op cit, pp71-72; J C Davis, 'The Levellers and Christianity', op cit, pp228-230; D M Wolfe (ed), op cit, p410; G H Sabine (ed), op cit, pp509, 534, 589.

81 *Tyranipocrit*, op cit, pp19, 36, 49, 51, 52.

Gerald Aylmer, in stressing the differences between Levellers and Diggers and the comparative isolation of the latter, observes that 'the nearest approach to Winstanley's ideas is found in the anonymous *Tyranipocrit* of August 1649... It is certainly a remarkable work...which advocates the relative equalisation of incomes, but even here we do not find open support for common ownership'.[82] But common ownership is no more than 'the extreme case of redistribution of wealth'.[83] Both common ownership and equalisation of incomes would have involved the expropriation of the rich and massive redistribution; both would have involved the destruction of the existing economic, social and political order; both were wholly revolutionary. The far left may be defined, therefore, in terms of the broad aspiration for the redistribution of wealth, which embraced both Digger communism and *Tyranipocrit's* equalisation of incomes, as well as the advocacy by Coppe and Foster of the expropriation of the rich and redistribution of their wealth to the poor. It was the defining principle of the far left and divided them from the leadership of the Levellers, Fifth Monarchists and Quakers.

It was a perfectly orthodox view that god had given the earth and its fruits to mankind and that in the beginning it held them in common. Although some thinkers did argue to the contrary that private property existed from the beginning and had been enacted by god, 'everyone agreed that whatever the earliest form of ownership had been, private property was now the norm, and that it was fully justified.' Common ownership did not have eternal validity and it had been found convenient to replace it with private property: 'that all things being divided, every man should know his own; otherwise no peace or concord could be maintained in human society.' In the first days of mankind the population was small enough for there to be more than sufficient lands and goods for everyone, but as population increased there was competition and contention and it was thought meet to set out the bounds of each one's ownership. This was prescribed by the 'law of nations'—the practices of civilised societies. 'By the Law of Nature all things were common', wrote Sir John Davies, but 'then came in the Law of Nations, which did limit the Law of Nature, and brought in property'.[84] This is why the appeals of the Levellers to the law of nature and to natural rights appeared as threats to private property.

---

82   G E Aylmer, 'The Religion of Gerrard Winstanley', in J F McGregor and B Reay (eds), op cit, pp114-115.
83   N Z Davis, *Society and Culture in Early Modern France* (London, 1975), p36.
84   J P Sommerville, *Politics and Ideology in England, 1603-1640* (Harlow, 1986), pp145-147.

The Leveller leaders, however, sought to place a constitutional bar on parliament 'abolishing property, levelling men's estates, or making all things common', and Lilburne condemned 'the erroneous tenets' of the Diggers.[85] They were anxious to counter the impression created by the sobriquet 'Levellers', which had been foisted on their party by their enemies in order to brand them as enemies of property, and to avoid being confused with the Diggers who called themselves the 'true levellers'. But a better informed and more subtle critic of the Levellers wrote:

> There has been a good while a rumour of a pestilence that walks in darkness, and has been known to have infected some that frequent your meetings, and are accounted as your own; and this rumour is not a whispering, it has spoken almost as loud as some of your cries for bread, and 'tis the doctrine of parity or levelling, bringing all men's estates to an equality... And however the crowd of those that follow you intend no such thing, but think these [the Levellers' proposals] are ways to secure their own property, yet just suspicion is upon many of you, and 'tis not your bare denial will serve.[86]

The finger may be pointed at Leveller supporters in Buckinghamshire, who invoked in December 1648 the 'golden rule or law, which we call equity: the sum of which is, saith Jesus, whatsoever you would that men should do to you, do to them, this is the Law and the Prophets', and declared that at the beginning:

> All men being alike privileged by birth, so all men were to enjoy the creatures alike without property one more than the other, all men by the grant of god are alike free...that is to say, no man was to lord or command over his own kind, neither to enclose the creatures to his own use, to the impoverishing of his neighbours, see the Charter, Genesis 1 from the 26th verse to the end of the chapter, and see the renewing of the Charter to Noah and his sons, Genesis 9 from the first verse to the 18th. But man following his own sensuality became a devourer of the creatures, and an encloser, not content that another should enjoy the same privilege as himself, but encloses all from his brother, so that all the land, trees, beasts, fish, fowl, etc are enclosed into a few mercenary hands, and all the rest deprived and made their slaves.[87]

85 W Haller and G Davies (eds), *The Leveller Tracts 1647-1653* (1944, reprinted Gloucester, Massachusetts, 1964), pp153, 327, 449.
86 W Haller and G Davies (eds), op cit, pp130-131.
87 G H Sabine (ed), op cit, pp611-612.

The Levellers of the Chiltern Hills, meeting at Aylesbury early in May 1649, attacked nobility, gentry and 'extorting lords of manors', as well as lawyers and episcopalian clergy, and declared their sympathy for the Diggers. They said they would support the poor in forming communes on the wastes and commons, 'in god's way, as those [in] Acts 2':

> We desire to go by the golden rule of equity, viz: 'To do to all men as we would they should do to us', and no otherwise; and as we would tyrannise over none, so we shall not suffer ourselves to be slaves to any whosoever.[88]

Accusations were made against one Leveller leader that he was sympathetic to communism or at least to a more equal distribution of wealth:

> This Mr Walwyn, to work upon the indigent and poorer sort of people, and to raise their spirits in discontents and clamours, etc did one time profess, he could wish with all his heart that there was neither pale, hedge nor ditch in the whole nation, and that it was an unconscionable thing that one man should have ten thousand pounds, and another more deserving and useful to the commonwealth, should not be worth two pence, or to that purpose. At another time discoursing of the inequality and disproportion of the estates and conditions of men in the world, had words to this purpose, that it was a sad and miserable thing that it should so continue and that it would never be well until all things were common.[89]

Walwyn did not flatly deny the statements attributed to him, and his reply was oblique and ambiguous:

> And as for riches, Saint James, whom I am exceeding in love with, had no great good opinion thereof: he demands positively, do not rich men oppress you... Nay, is there not such an expression again in Scripture, as, go to, weep and howl, you rich men?... And where you charge me, that I find fault that some abound, whilst others want bread; truly, I think it a sad thing, in so fruitful a land as through god's blessing this is; and I do think it one main end of government to provide that those who refuse not labour should eat comfortably.

In a tract of 1643, in which he dwelt on the contrast between the

88   Ibid, pp643-647.
89   W Haller and G Davies (eds), op cit, pp302-303.

deprivations of the poor and the abundance of the well to do, he added:

> What is here aimed at?... Would you have all things common? For love seeks not her own good, but the good of others. You say very true, it is the Apostles' doctrine, and you may remember the multitude of believers had all things common.

Nevertheless, he declared his solidarity with the declarations of the other Leveller leaders that under their proposed constitution parliament would not have the power to 'level men's estates, destroy property, or make all things common'. He signed, and probably penned, the manifesto of 14 April 1649 in which the Leveller leaders repeated their denial that they intended 'an equalling of men's estates', or ever had it in their thoughts to do so, for that would be 'most injurious, unless there did precede an universal assent thereunto from all and everyone of the people', and it was for that reason they denied to parliament the power to do it on its own authority. However, this was followed by a consideration of apostolic communism, which they said was voluntary and not a requirement for Christians, it being limited to a special period in the history of Christianity:

> The community amongst the primitive Christians was voluntary, not coactive; they brought their goods and laid them at the apostles' feet, they were not enjoined to bring them, it was the effect of their charity and heavenly mindedness, which the blessed apostles begot in them, and not the injunction of any constitution, which as it was but for a short time done, and in but two or three places, that the Scripture makes mention of, so does the very doing of it there and the apostles' answer to him that detained a part, imply that it was not esteemed a duty, but reckoned a voluntary act occasioned by the abundant measure of faith that was in those Christians and apostles.[90]

The Digger communes were similarly voluntary associations.[91] But clearly the issue of early Christian communism troubled the Leveller leaders and perhaps that was because they were aware of its influence on their supporters and other radicals.

Christopher Hill detects a right wing and a left wing in the Leveller

---

90   J R McMichael and B Taft (eds), op cit, pp41-42, 49-50, 80, 337-338, 417-419; A L Morton, *The World of the Ranters*, op cit, pp183-186.

91   M Goldsmith, 'Levelling by Sword, Spade and Word: Radical Egalitarianism in the English Revolution', in C Jones, M Newitt and S Roberts (eds), *Politics and People in Revolutionary England* (Oxford, 1986), p77.

movement, with the latter being 'less concerned with constitutional issues, more with economics, with defending the poor against the rich, the common people against great men—which one suspects were the chief issues in the minds of the poorer classes in the late 1640s.' And · a preacher in 1650 said that 'the multitude still much incline to a popular parity, a levelling anarchy'.[92] A critic of the Levellers recognised that they did not intend 'parity or levelling, bringing all men's estates to an equality', but nevertheless warned them: 'Confide not in your present intentions... There is not the most clear and candid soul amongst you that knows to what (now abhorred) actions he may be driven by the violence of the people, if that sea shall once break over his banks, and 'twill not be then in their power to stop'.[93] This was a good reason for supporting the Cromwellian dictatorship.

Demands for the redistribution of wealth surfaced amongst the Fifth Monarchists. Morgan Llwyd visualised a great redistribution of land, so that 'no poor men should have too little, nor the rich too much.' But Capp concludes that the Fifth Monarchists did not support common ownership, and many of them defended private property. He judges their programme of reforms was attractive to small producers.[94] Reay considers that in the sort of society envisaged by the Quakers 'there would have been some redistribution of wealth'. 'You wallow yourselves in the earth's treasure like swine in the mire', Ben Nicholson told the gentry, 'and never consider that the earth is the Lord's...and that he has given it to the sons of men in general, and not to a few lofty ones which lord it over their brethren'. But Reay concludes: 'The Quakers were not communists: they probably had in mind a nation of small producers, with some limitations on the accumulation of wealth'.[95] Similarities are marked between Levellers, Fifth Monarchists and Quakers in their programmes and in the social composition of their support. Reduction of the extremes of wealth and poverty was probably favoured by small producers in general, but also most vitally the continuation of private property.[96]

The dilemma of the revolutionary strata of the 'middle sort of people' was perhaps encapsulated in the thinking of Peter Cornelius Plockhoy, a Dutch Mennonite who came to England shortly before the death of Cromwell and remained to participate in the revival of radical agitation

92 C Hill, *The World Turned Upside Down*, op cit, pp91-99, 193.
93 W Haller and G Davies (eds), op cit, pp130-131.
94 B Capp, op cit, pp166-167.
95 B Reay, *The Quakers*, op cit, pp39-40.
96 A Soboul, op cit, ch II.

in 1659. His plan was a way forward for the 'middle sort'. As Davis notes, his pre-eminent concern was with inequality: 'The escape from inequality was focal to building a new society'. His aim was to offer an escape from:

> the yoke of the temporal and spiritual Pharaohs, who have long enough domineered over our bodies and souls, and set up again (as in former times) righteousness, love and brotherly sociableness, which are scarce anywhere to be found, for the convincing of those that place all great-ness only in domineering, and not in well doing, contrary to the pat-tern and doctrine of the Lord Jesus, who came not to be served but to serve... In direct opposition and contradiction to the world where they are accounted the greatest who have the most servants, and not they that do most service to others, and therefore the world's greatness and the greatness of Christians differ as light and darkness, whereas true Christians being merciful do endeavour to ease men's burdens, instead thereof others...are still making the burden heavier.

His model was early Christianity when Christ:

> instituted a partnership or society of mutual love by the denomination of brethren, abolishing amongst his disciples all pre-eminency or dom-ineering of one over another, requiring that the gifts and means of sub-sistence in the world (for necessity and delight) should be common, having called his people to a moderation and to a life suitable to pure nature, so that all Christendom ought to be merely a certain great fra-ternity consisting of such as (having denied the world and their own lusts) conspire together in Christ, the sole head and spring of love, doing well to one another, and for his sake distribute their goods to those that stand in need.

He invited voluntary withdrawal from the world into a co-operative society, involving the pooling of resources and communal living in a simple style, but continuing to participate in the economy of the world, and the profits of their work in agriculture, manufacture and trade going to the society for communal purposes. There would be equality between the members of the society—'no one exalts itself, nor ac-counts itself worthier than other'—and there would be no exploitation. But the significant point is that membership is to be restricted to hus-bandmen, craftsmen, tradesmen, mariners, teachers and physicians, and is to exclude unskilled labourers and the poor in general—the very people for whom the far left utopias were designed, well illustrating the divorce between the 'middle sort' and the poor. The economic ac-tivities of the society would be made profitable in competition with the outside world by bulk purchasing, large scale production, and lower costs resulting from communal living. The insecurities of life would be reduced by the support of the society for the young and the old, for the sick and for widows and orphans. Davis rightly points out that the difficulty, with which Plockhoy wrestled, was to maintain an egalitarian community within a world dominated by great inequalities and a market economy. Eduard Bernstein, who devoted a chapter to Plockhoy, described his utopia as 'a socialistic community with limited private property', and one in which he strove to reconcile private property with cooperation instead of competition. He considered him a pioneer of the cooperative movement. In 1663 Plockhoy tried to establish his society within the Dutch colony of New Netherland in North America but it was destroyed by English military occupation.[97]

This may be taken as representing the dilemma of the revolutionary strata of the 'middling sort' in the 1650s. Faced with their failure to take full control of the state and society, they could separate, just as the religious radicals separated from the established church, and form a society within a society, governed by their own ideals and rules, but still operating economically within the larger society. Or they could remain in the larger society, compromise and cooperate with the old ruling class and, under their political leadership and social hegemony, seek to continue the development of a market economy and capitalist enterprise. The 'middling sort' chose to follow the latter course and to sacrifice their ideals of equality and brotherhood, which in any case excluded the unskilled labourers and the poor. Plockhoy's thinking, with its attempt to come to terms with the economic imperatives of the advancing economies of Holland and England, relates more closely to the way society was developing than Winstanley's thinking.

God and revolution

The far left revolutionaries invoked god and the Bible as the authorities for their demands. This might seem to support the view of the revisionists that the revolution was all about religion, but it is necessary to ask the questions, 'What religion? Whose religion?' The rich, said

---

97 P Cornelius [Plockhoy], *A Way Propounded to Make the Poor in these and Other Nations Happy* (London, 1659); E Bernstein, *Cromwell and Communism: Socialism and Democracy in the Great English Revolution*, translated by H J Stenning, ch XV (1930, reprinted London, 1963); J C Davis, *Utopia and the Ideal Society: A Study of English Utopian Writing, 1516-1700* (Cambridge, 1981), pp331-338.

Tyranipocrit, have built churches and lavishly ornamented them with 'preposterous offerings' to god, but god would have wished that these resources had been given to the poor instead.[98] The central ritual of Christian churches was the eucharist or communion, but Winstanley said that the true communion was not eating a little bread and drinking a little wine in a church service, it was 'eating and drinking in love and sweet communion one with another from house to house'.[99] Coppe put it more brutally:

> Why after a consecration…eating a bit of bread and drinking a sip of wine perhaps once a month, why mother of mischief is this communion? O thou flattering and deceitful tongue, god shall root thee out of the land of the living. Is this communion? No, no, mother of witchcrafts! The true communion amongst men is to have all things common, and call nothing one hath, one's own. And the true external breaking of bread is to eat bread together in singleness of heart, and to break thy bread to the hungry, and tell them it's their own bread, etc else your religion is in vain.[100]

In order to challenge a ruling class which based its authority on a religion which taught that the existing social hierarchy was ordained by god, a god who instructed the poor to accept their poverty and their subordinate place in society, and to defer to those set over them, it was necessary for the far left revolutionaries to authorise the subversion of the existing order and the turning of the world upside down (or in their view turning the world the right way up), by revealing the truth which had been concealed from the people about god's true intentions for the world, and freeing them from acquiescence in the falsified religion of the ruling class. This meant preaching 'practical Christianity', equality, and redistribution of wealth.

What places these far left revolutionaries firmly in the prehistory of socialism, however, is that their revolution was to be accomplished by divide intervention. 'The Lord himself will do this great work', wrote Winstanley, 'without either sword or weapon': 'So that this work is not done by wars, counsels, or hands of men'; 'the arm of the Lord only shall bring these mighty things to pass'.[101] This was echoed by Coppe: 'This levelling…shall up, not by sword, not by might, etc but by my spirit, says the Lord'; it will be accomplished not 'by material sword, by

---

98 *Tyranipocrit*, op cit, p10.
99 G H Sabine (ed), op cit, pp141-143.
100 N Smith (ed), op cit, pp114-115.
101 G H Sabine (ed), op cit, pp153, 182, 205.

human might, power, or strength, but by the pure spirit of universal love, who is god'.[102] It is not hard to detect here a sense of the weakness of the poor in the face of the strength of their rulers, who controlled government both nationally and locally, and commanded the wealth and resources of society, backed at this time by a powerful standing army.

The parliamentarian party of the civil war was infused with millenarianism—expectation of the defeat of Antichrist and the establishment of Christ's kingdom on earth—and the revolutionary fervour of the late 1640s and early 1650s came from belief in the imminence of the millennium.[103] As Davis observes, millenarianism 'affected the thinking and aspirations of a whole generation—the generation coming to maturity in the 1640s'. It was no longer merely a matter of academic speculation or the beliefs of a few crackpots. It was a popular belief. What the left did was to inject it with social revolutionary implications.[104] Popular dreams of an ideal society merged with millenarianism, thus fusing the secular and earthly with the spiritual and religious, and dreams which had held out no means of achievement now found an answer in the Second Coming of Jesus Christ.

A L Morton focused his study of the 'utopia of the folk' on the fantasy of 'the land of Cokaygne', which appears for the first time in Europe in the 13th century (the name is probably derived from 'kuchen' or cake). An English poem described it as a land of plenty which all could enjoy without the need to work, a land 'of eternal youth and eternal summer, of joy, fellowship, and peace'. For people struggling through endless back breaking labour to obtain barely sufficient to eat, it was an image so appropriate that it persisted through centuries in numberless versions in many different countries, even into the popular music of the 20th century.[105] Bernard Capp argues that 'the arcadian dream of harmonious peace in a bountiful environment and the earthly, sensual peasant paradise known as the Land of Cockaygne' probably contributed to popular conceptions of the millennium, in which there would be harmony and peace, plenty and leisure, good health and long life. He places the millenarianism of the Fifth Monarchists in the context of this popular culture:

An age of boundless prosperity and plenty was a recurring theme in

102 N Smith (ed), op cit, pp89, 110.
103 C Hill, *Antichrist in Seventeenth-Century England*, op cit, ch III.
104 J C Davis, *Utopia and the Ideal Society*, op cit, p33.
105 A L Morton, *The English Utopia*, op cit, ch I; F Graus, 'Social Utopias in the Middle Ages', *Past and Present*, 38 (1967), pp6-10.

millennial writings from Brightman to Fifth Monarchist pamphlets and popular chapbooks, and even writers who laid most stress on spiritual blessings added guarantees of worldly wealth. Creature comforts would be readily provided. Houses would be solid and comfortable, food and drink abundant... It is easy to see how New Jerusalem and the Land of Cockaygne could merge. In the millennium, as in Cockaygne, the grinding toil of the labourer would cease.[106]

The same dream of the ideal society inspired Winstanley before he launched the Digger communes. It would be 'a land flowing with milk and honey, plenty of all things'. 'There shall be no barrenness in the earth or cattle, for they shall bring forth abundantly.' The earth shall be free 'from thorns, and briars, and barrenness; the air and winds from unseasonable storms and distempers.' There will be 'no poor', 'no beggars, no tears, no complaining, no oppression... Then our swords shall be beaten into plough irons, and our spears into pruning hooks.' 'None shall desire to have more than another, or to be lord over other.' 'There shall be no need of lawyers, prisons, or engines of punishment.' Thomas Venner, the Fifth Monarchist, had a similar vision of the millennium.[107] These were fantasies in the 17th century but they might be seen as containing the message that socialism cannot succeed unless it brings prosperity, equally distributed.

Resistance

Reliance on divine intervention, however, was not incompatible with action to inaugurate the social transformation, not only action in the form of writing tracts and manifestos to communicate god's message, but more demonstrative actions as well, for god worked through human agents. Abiezer Coppe went to London and Southwark in 1649 and stood in the streets protesting at the rich as they passed in their coaches, 'with his hand fiercely stretched out, his hat cocked up', staring at them as if he 'would look through them', gnashing his teeth at them, 'and day and night with a huge loud voice proclaiming the day of the Lord'. Then he fell to the ground and kissed the feet of beggars, blind and sick persons, acting out his doctrine of equality. He did this for 12 or 13 days, attracting much attention and a 'great multitude following

106 B Capp, 'The Fifth Monarchists and Popular Millenarianism', in J F McGregor and B Reay (eds), op cit, pp176, 185-189.

107 G H Sabine (ed), op cit, pp169, 181, 183, 186, 204; W Medley, *A Standard Set Up* (1657).

him up and down'.[108] This piece of street theatre was the equivalent of modern protesters seeking by dramatic actions to draw the attention of people, and particularly the media, to their cause.

Great importance was attached to symbols, and symbolic actions were influential both in upholding and in defying the social order. Everyday rituals in manners, speech and body language reveal the existence of class distinctions. In early modern society the deference of social subordinates to their superiors was marked by baring of heads, standing, bowing, curtseying and addressing them with terms of respect. Consciously, unconsciously or habitually these were acknowledgements of the superiority of their masters, which were taught to inferiors from childhood and became ingrained in their natures.[109] In Tudor and Stuart society hats were 'for ever being doffed and donned to emphasise the complex hierarchy of ranks and authorities. Everyone, every day, many times a day, by removing his hat or putting it on, gave visible proof of his acceptance of the great principle of subordination universally at work' at the royal court and in the aristocratic household, in the family, in the villages and in the towns, in the schools and in the universities.[110] Refusal to remove the hat was a defiance of superior authority or superior rank and an assertion of equality. 'If a poor man come before a rich man', wrote a Quaker in 1655, 'it may be the rich man will move his hat, that is called courtesy and humility; but the poor man must stand with his hat off before him, and that is called honour and manners, and due respect to him'.[111] When the leaders of the first Digger commune—Winstanley and Everard—appeared before General Fairfax at Whitehall in 1649 to give an explanation of their occupation of St George's Hill in Surrey, they refused to remove their hats. They defended their 'discourtesy' by saying that Fairfax 'was but their fellow creature'; 'that all men are equal, that they are not to stand bare to any, not to the General, being not his servants', adding with down to earth practicality 'that they brought their hats to wear on their heads, and not to hold in their hands'.[112] Bulstrode Whitelocke recorded this 'more largely' in his memoirs 'because it was the beginning of the appearance of this opinion, and that we might the better understand and avoid these weak persuasions'.[113] He was wrong on the first point

108 N Smith (ed), op cit, pp97, 105.
109 J Walter, 'The Impact on Society: A World Turned Upside Down?' in J Morrill (ed), The Impact of the English Civil War (London, 1991), pp115.
110 L Stone, The Crisis of the Aristocracy 1558-1641 (Oxford, 1965), pp34-35.
111 B Reay, The Quakers, op cit, p140.
112 A Perfect Diurnall (16-23 April 1649); Perfect Occurrences (20-27 April 1649).
113 B Whitelocke, Memorials of the English Affairs (London, 1682), pp383-384.

because it was a long established gesture of protest, which had been practised by Lilburne, but right about the second because it was adopted by the Quakers to assert their belief in the equality of all before god.

The Quakers also addressed their superiors with the term of familiarity 'thou' rather than the term of formality 'you'. They said that 'amongst the great and rich ones of the earth, they will either *thou* or *you* one another if they be equal in degree, as they call it; but if a man of low degree in the earth come to speak to any of them, then he must *you* the rich man, but the rich man will *thou* him'.[114] Thomas Fuller wrote in 1651:

> We maintain that *thou* from superiors to inferiors is proper, as a sign of command; from equals to equals is passable, as a note of familiarity; but from inferiors to superiors, if proceeding from ignorance, has a smack of clownishness; if from affectation, a tang of contempt... Such who now quarrel at the honour will hereafter question the wealth of others. Such as now accuse them for ambition for being higher, will hereafter condemn them for covetousness, for being broader than others; yea, and produce Scripture too, proper and pregnant enough for their purpose as abused by their interpretation.

Unless they were repressed, 'such as now introduce thou and thee will (if they can) expel mine and thine, dissolving all property into confusion'. The same assertions of equality reappeared in the French Revolution.[115]

The formative influence on the left was the realisation that their enemies were not just the king, courtiers and bishops, but the ruling class and its institutions (parliament itself, the law courts and local government). The Levellers powerfully expressed and focused this realisation between 1646 and 1649.[116] Parliament, said *Tyranipocrit*, was composed of members of the ruling class, who did not 'know the poor man's wants, because they were never poor themselves'. The Long Parliament initially took away 'some small abuses', but the 'old tyrannies' were not removed 'so that the poor people might have had liberty and wealth... There was no care taken for them that had most need of help, which were the poor people, that wanted food and raiment; but the king and parliament fell at odds concerning the militia', and the civil war was fought between two lots of aspiring tyrants to decide which would exercise the tyranny.[117]

114 B Reay, *The Quakers*, op cit, p140.
115 C Hill, *The World Turned Upside Down*, op cit, pp198-199.
116 B Manning, *The English People and the English Revolution* (1976, London, second edition with new introduction, 1991), ch 9.
117 *Tyranipocrit*, op cit, pp53-54.

Similarly, Walwyn told the people:

The king, parliament, great men in the city and army, have made you but the stairs by which they have mounted to honour, wealth and power. The only quarrel that has been, and at present is but this, namely, whose slaves the people shall be.[118]

'The rich covetous oppressing men', wrote George Fox the Younger, 'have the only power to choose lawmakers, and they will choose...such as will uphold them in their oppression; and the poor man...must be subject to the laws which they make who are his oppressors'.[119] Laurence Clarkson, in his Leveller phase, warned the people:

Your oppressions and divisions came by those that you have chosen to ease you... Have you not chosen oppressors to redeem you from oppression?... For reason affirms, so long as you choose such as you say are your lords...injustice will continue, oppression will reign.[120]

Hertfordshire Levellers announced that they would not 'choose...for a parliament man...lords of manors, impropriators [lay owners of tithes], and lawyers, whose interest is in our oppression and at this day keep us in bondage like Egyptian taskmasters'.[121]

Clarkson urged the lower order to elect representatives from their own class, 'such that are your equals', if they ever wanted to see improvement in their condition.[122] *Tyranipocrit* continued:

Now if there be any such persons in the parliament that has not in his able age laboured, so as god commands all men, then turn him out and choose an honest labouring man in his place, for none but such persons that have laboured according to god's law are fit to make and maintain laws, and if any other men do make injunctions and call them laws, as they do, no man is bound to obey them, because god is the supreme lawmaker, and therefore when men will not obey god's law, then they lose all their ruling power.[123]

Nothing came of this. Most of the poor were excluded from the franchise and the Levellers did not see their way to change that, because

118 J R McMichael and B Taft (eds), op cit, p306.
119 Quoted in W Schenk, op cit, p125.
120 Quoted in B Reay, 'Lawrence Clarkson: An Artisan and the English Revolution', in C Hill, B Reay and W Lamont (eds), *The World of the Muggletonians* (London, 1983), pp174-175.
121 W Schenk, op cit, p66.
122 B Reay, 'Lawrence Clarkson', op cit, pp174-175.
123 *Tyranipocrit*, op cit, p48.

they feared that they would not cast their votes independently from their masters and employers. Yet so long as the economic and social power of the landlords and rich merchants remained intact, and there was no secret ballot, the composition of parliament would not change.

Winstanley was not content to rest with the propaganda of the word but undertook soon the propaganda of deeds:

> Yet my mind was not at rest, because nothing was acted, and thoughts run in me, that words and writings were all nothing, and must die, for action is the life of all, and if you do not act, you do nothing. Within a little time I was made obedient to the word [of god] in that particular likewise; for I took up my spade and went and broke the ground upon George-hill in Surrey.[124]

Thus he inaugurated the Digger communes as models of a society in which there would be no rich and poor, no paying of rents to landlords, no working for wages, no buying and selling, but all would work cooperatively to till the land, which they would hold in common, and share their produce according to need. They were forcibly dispersed by local landlords and well to do farmers.[125] Digger communes appeared briefly at perhaps ten or more different locations scattered over several counties, and though the active support they attracted was tiny, there may have been many more passive sympathisers.[126] The fact that the first settlement was imitated in a number of other places spread over a wide area indicated its potential to initiate a mass movement if it had not been quickly snuffed out. John Gurney demonstrates that at Cobham Winstanley did gain a degree of support from local people, and he concludes that 'given the right local conditions' his ideas 'could find a receptive audience in rural communities'.[127]

The Diggers visualised a dual system in which communal ownership would be voluntary and would coexist alongside private ownership of land. Winstanley spelt out in the *Law of Freedom* that the system of collective production would take place on what he called the commonwealth's land—monastic lands which had been expropriated at the Reformation, crown lands, bishops' lands, and common and waste lands—these would be settled by 'all that are willing to come in to the practice of this government, and be obedient to the laws

---

124 G H Sabine (ed), op cit, pp315-316.
125 B Manning, *1649: The Crisis of the English Revolution* (London, 1992), pp109-132.
126 K Thomas, 'Another Digger Broadside', *Past and Present*, 42 (1969).
127 J Gurney, 'Gerrard Winstanley and the Digger Movement in Walton and Cobham', *Historical Journal*, vol 37 (1994).

thereof; and for others, who are not willing, let them stay in the way of buying and selling...till they be willing'.[128] But Davis thinks that Winstanley was not against enclosure because he said that the 'lords of manors and gentry ought to have their enclosure lands free to them without molestation'. Winstanley used the term 'enclosures', however, to mean land held as private property as opposed to common property, and he refers to the private sector sometimes as enclosed land and sometimes as the part where buying and selling would continue. Davis misses the point that what the Diggers were opposing was the enclosure of the common and waste lands, which was the central issue in agrarian relations at that time. The fundamental question, which the Diggers highlighted, was whether the common and waste lands would be brought under more intensive cultivation by privatisation or by common ownership. And the Diggers intended to exert pressure to persuade the private owners to surrender to common ownership.

The significance of the Diggers was that they did not rely only on divide intervention to bring the whole nation into line with their model communes. They believed themselves to be carrying out the will of god, but god required human action. They did not intend to overthrow the power of the landlords and big farmers by force or to expropriate their estates. During the course of their struggle and as a result of their experience they evolved two strategies to bring about piecemeal the progressive collapse of the existing system. Both of these strategies projected mass popular action, and, as Petegorsky observes, social change was to be initiated 'through the direct action of politically conscious individuals'—the example of the occupiers of St George's Hill—rousing the masses to effect their own emancipation.[129] The first strategy was that the Diggers called upon 'all labourers, or such as are called poor people' to cease to work for landlords and large farmers.[130] The way to end the domination of the latter was not to thrust them out by force but for the people to refuse to work for them any longer. The rich derived their wealth from the labour of the poor and the withdrawal of that labour would pull down the rich. Winstanley addressed the lords of manors and their big tenants: 'What would you do if you had not such labouring men to work for you?'[131] Large estates and farms which depended on

---

128 G H Sabine (ed), op cit, pp513, 557-558; J C Davis, *Utopia and the Ideal Society*, op cit, pp183-185.
129 D W Petegorsky, *Left-Wing Democracy in the English Civil War* (1940, reprinted London, 1996), pp199-200.
130 G H Sabine (ed), op cit, p262.
131 Ibid, pp195-196, 262, 363, 656-657.

hired labour would cease to be economically viable, and their owners would be reduced to living off only such land as they could tend with their own and their family's labour. The assumption was that then they would be constrained to give up private ownership and merge their lands with the Digger communes. As Christopher Hill says: 'The Digger colony on St George's Hill was intended to be the first stage in a sort of general strike against wage labour.' 'The essence of the digging experiment', writes J C Davis, 'was therefore the withdrawal of labour from employment on the estates of landlords and rich tenant farmers.' 'It was not expropriation', adds Hill, 'but it would have amounted to piecemeal deprivation of the profits of ownership'.[132] If it did not result in the owners giving up private ownership, at the very least it would have the effect of reducing inequality and limiting the accumulation of wealth. It also presupposed that the striking labourers would join the Digger communes in order to get a livelihood.

The second strategy was that the Diggers called on tenants to stop paying rents. 'He that works for another, either for wages, or to pay him rent, works unrighteously': '*Let Israel go free*; break in pieces quickly the band of particular property, disown this oppressing murder, oppressing and thievery of buying and selling of land, owning of landlords and paying of rents.' Robert Coster, the Digger poet, wrote:

> If the lords of manors, and other gentlemen who covet after so much land, could not let it out by parcels, but must be constrained to keep it in their own hands, then would they want those great bags of money (which do maintain pride, idleness, and fulness of bread) which are carried into them by their tenants... If the lords of manors, and other gentlemen, had not got those great bags of money brought into them, then down would fall the lordliness of their spirits, and then poor men might speak to them; then there might be an acknowledging of one another to be fellow creatures. For what is the reason that great gentlemen covet after so much land? Is it not because farmers and others creep to them in a slavish manner, proffering them great sums of money for such and such parcels of it, which does give them an occasion to tyrannise over their fellow creatures which they call their inferiors?[133]

132 C Hill, 'Pottage for Freeborn Englishmen: Attitudes to Wage Labour', *Change and Continuity in Seventeenth-Century England* (London, 1974), p233; 'The Religion of Gerrard Winstanley', *Past and Present*, Supplement 5 (1980), pp26-27; 'Winstanley and Freedom', in R C Richardson and G M Ridden (eds), *Freedom in the English Revolution* (Manchester, 1986), p158; J C Davis, *Utopia and the Ideal Society*, op cit, pp185-187; T Kenyon, *Utopian Communism and Political Thought in Early Modern England* (London, 1989), pp165-167, 176-177.
133 G H Sabine (ed), op cit, pp262, 264, 411-413, 657.

According to Digger theory the existing system had been imposed by the Norman Conquest, but this had been overcome by the defeat of the king in the civil war, and so copyhold tenures—customary tenures whose abolition was demanded by many on the left—were extinguished and copyhold tenants were no longer obliged to pay rents and dues to lords of manors:

> The tenants of copyholds are freed from obedience to their lords of manors... Neither can the lords of manors compel their tenants of copyholds to come to their court barons, nor to be of their juries, nor take an oath to be true to them, nor to pay fines [on entering into the tenancy], heriots [on the death of the tenant], quit-rent, nor any homage, as formerly while the king and lords were in their power. And if the tenants stand up to maintain their freedom against their lords' oppressing power, the tenants forfeit nothing but are protected.[134]

By this strategy the manorial system would have collapsed, indeed feudalism would have been finally extinguished, and the nobility and gentry would have been deprived of a great deal of their wealth and power. Winstanley identified copyholders with the smaller peasants. But individually they would not have been protected by Winstanley's theory that it would be lawful for them to withhold their rents; they would have been protected only if the mass of them did this simultaneously. The combination of a labour strike and a rent strike would have accomplished an economic and social revolution, but it would have required a vast amount of organisation and a legion of local leaders, far beyond the capacity of the small band of Diggers, and there would still have been questions about the control of state power.

The idea of strike action existed at the time of the English Revolution. John Sanders had been a prosperous master ironmonger but was reduced to working as a poor nailer at Harborne, near Birmingham. He combined millenarianism with royalism and Anglicanism—a warning, as Capp says, against 'imposing rigid categories on the mid-century flux of ideas'. He set himself up as a prophet—'herald or ambassador from the great kingly power and parliament of heaven'—and appeared in 1655 in the streets of Birmingham dressed in rags and with a carpenter's rule in his hand, and addressed the ironmongers and the nailers. He told the ironmongers to remember their origins: 'Many of you were poor, but now being raised up in the world you have forgotten god.' The 'rich, covetous and uncharitable ironmongers grind the faces of the

---

134 Ibid, pp411-412, 510.

poor whom the Lord has promised to deliver for his name's sake.' He urged them to make a practical repentance by increasing the prices they paid the nailers for their products, 'that they may not have cause to hate you, many hundreds of them enjoying nothing but misery and want'. He told the nailers:

> Brethren and fellow sufferers, if this be not forthwith done, for healing of your grievances, then take my counsel, let them work themselves; for certainly you that make the ware are the most, and most considerable, though least valued and worst provided for... Do you poor labouring tradesmen hold together, by assisting and maintaining one another one fortnight or a month, and forbear working for the cunning Egyptian taskmasters now in the spring. However take my advice and let us have a general meeting thereupon. If we cannot gain our desires, we will try another way, that is, I will draw a petition to the Lord Protector for a corporation, that we may make orders among ourselves; and those that have set up our trade within these seven or eight years (not having served just apprenticeships) may be called in question.[135]

It is not known whether anything came of this, probably nothing. The conflict was between merchants and small producers, and one in which the former were extending their control over the industry and reducing the latter to their employees. Sanders' second solution was the typical defensive response of small producers, which was to seek the protection of a guild and the enforcement of the seven year apprenticeship in order to prevent the ironmongers from employing large amounts of cheap unapprenticed labour. The case of Sanders illustrates the way in which millenarianism was rooted in the real life of the poor.

In 1654 the keelmen of Newcastle upon Tyne struck against their low wages. The mayor and other magistrates of the town sought to mediate but they did not satisfy the demands of the men who in the end were forced back to work by a troop of horse and a company of foot from the army. There was further trouble in 1660. This time the keelmen blocked the passage of the river with their boats, but once again the army was employed to break the blockade. This was the beginning of a long history of industrial action by the keelmen. They were wage earners engaged in a capitalist industry and pioneered 'a new step in

---

135 W H B Court, *The Rise of the Midland Industries 1600-1838* (Oxford, 1938), pp62-63;
    B Capp, 'The Fifth Monarchists and Popular Millenarianism', op cit, pp184, 187.

the direction of modern industrial organisation'.[136]

These cases demonstrate the difficulties of organising industrial action at this stage of economic development. Levine and Wrightson contrast the absence of industrial action by the coalminers with the militancy of the keelmen:

> The miners were both fragmented into independent working units and geographically dispersed. They had less occasion to formulate a collective sense of grievance, or to express it in large scale action, than the keelmen, who were employed by a limited number of Newcastle fitters, worked the river together, lived near one another for the most part, and very often shared a Scottish origin.[137]

Court explained as follows the failure of the nailers to organise and take collective action:

> They worked under conditions which made organisation always difficult. Scattered and separated over miles of country in their nail shops; too poorly paid to support attempts to ensure that they should be paid better; above all, following a trade easily picked up and entered, whether for part time or full time; theirs was an industry without unity, strongly resembling in the general form of its organisation...the sweating trades of large cities of later times.[138]

Even in London, where the concentration of a large population formed the main base for popular radicalism, wage workers were scattered in very small numbers over separate workshops, segregated into very many different trades, and subjected to a face to face relationship with their employers, who exercised a patriarchal discipline over them.

One section of the labour force, however, did exhibit a remarkable degree of political consciousness—the apprentices in London and the young men who had just completed their terms of service and were working as wage earning journeymen. Throughout the revolution they petitioned and demonstrated and provided the main force of London mobs. They played crucial roles in bringing down the government of Charles I in 1641-42 and in the demise of the republic in 1659-60. It may be said that they moved with the shifting opinions of the 'middle sort', but they were not a monolithic political force, frequently being

---

136 J U Nef, *The Rise of the British Coal Industry*, vol II (2 vols, London, 1932), pp177-178; R Howell, *Newcastle upon Tyne and the Puritan Revolution* (Oxford, 1967), pp292-293; D Levine and K Wrightson, *The Making of an Industrial Society: Whickham 1560-1765* (Oxford, 1991), p391.

137 D Levine and K Wrightson, op cit, p392.

138 W H B Court, op cit, p138.

divided between radicals and conservatives.[139] It is clear that they saw themselves as representing youth: apprentices justified joining with journeymen in petitioning on the grounds that they were all young men, and sometimes they made overt reference to the generational differences between themselves and their masters. Indeed when contemporaries described crowds as consisting of 'apprentices' they often meant that they were composed of boys and young men.[140] There can be little question that they were exploited labour and they often made complaints about the way in which they were treated by their masters. The fact that many ran away and that half never completed their terms indicated no great satisfaction.[141] One of their petitions spoke of 'the hard usage and slavish bondage borne and endured by many apprentices and servants in this city and kingdom'.[142]

They were very different from the mass of wage earners. They came mainly from the 'middling sort', into which class they were destined to graduate. They did include a substantial minority of sons of gentry, but very few sons of labourers: in relation to the social structure at large, sons of gentry were over-represented and sons of labourers under-represented. They were an elite group, literate and open to be influenced by the ferment of ideas in revolutionary London. From the ranks of those who completed their terms would come the next generation of London merchants, shopkeepers and skilled artisans. They felt solidarity with other apprentices, but also a community of interest with the general body of the traders and craftsmen of the capital, with whose prosperity or otherwise their own futures were tied.[143] It is difficult to ascertain the extent to which apprentices were influenced by and followed the lead of their masters. Certainly there

139 S R Smith, 'The Apprentices Parliament of 1647', *History Today*, vol XXII (1972); 'The London Apprentices as 17th Century Adolescents', *Past and Present*, 61 (1973); 'Almost Revolutionaries: The London Apprentices during the Civil War', *The Huntington Library Quarterly*, vol XLII (1978-79).

140 *An Humble Declaration of the Apprentices and other Young Men of the City of London* (London, 1642/43); *The Humble Remonstrance of the Apprentices of the City of London* (London, 1647); P S Seaver, 'Declining Status in an Aspiring Age: The Problem of the Gentle Apprentice in Seventeenth-Century London', in B Y Kunze and D D Brautigan (eds), *Court, Country and Culture* (Rochester, New York, 1992), pp133-134; R B Manning, *Village Revolts: Social Protest and Popular Disturbances in England 1509-1640* (Oxford, 1988), p193.

141 A L Beier, 'Social Problems in Elizabethan London', in J Barry (ed), *The Tudor and Stuart Town* (London, 1990), pp132-133; P S Seaver, op cit, pp133-134; R H Hilton, op cit, pp109, 215.

142 *The Humble Remonstrance of the Apprentices of the City of London* (London, 1647).

143 M J Kitch, 'Capital and Kingdom: Migration to Later Stuart London', in A L Beier and R Finlay (eds), *London 1500-1700: The Making of the Metropolis* (London, 1986), pp225, 226, 246.

were many cases where masters and their apprentices were in accord in politics and religion, but there were also cases where masters and their apprentices took opposite sides in the civil war or where apprentices had different views on religion from their masters. Apprentices did act on their own initiatives in politics and religion and did prove difficult for their masters to control when as groups they intervened actively in politics and religion, showing capacity to organise themselves independently, and exhibiting solidarity among themselves in actions, sometimes violent actions.[144] Their repeated interventions in national politics defied the patriarchal order by which fathers or masters were deemed to be sole representatives of their households—wives, children, apprentices and servants. They justified themselves in terms which made revolutionary claims for the unenfranchised and for those excluded from political rights, to participate in national debates about the future of church and state.

They described themselves as 'the youngest and weakest of men' and 'the meanest members of this great commonwealth', but claimed that they were 'a part of this nation', 'fellow commoners'—though mere servants they were also subjects and had 'by birth a right of subsistence here'. Therefore they asserted that they were concerned about, and had an interest in, the condition of church and state, and the 'native and just fundamental rights' of the people; conceiving 'ourselves (in our proportion) to have as real an interest in the kingdom's enjoyments, as those who in respect of place or other accidents are above us'; holding that 'our share and part in either a well established or subverted government is of as much moment as any conditions of Englishmen whatsoever'; 'nor can we see any reason why a poor or illiterate man...should not seek for redress of his grievances as well as a rich and learned.' This was the rhetoric of both radical and conservative apprentices and journeymen.[145] There is some similarity here with the claims made by some women to justify their interventions in public affairs.[146] The role of the apprentices reflected, nevertheless, the domination of the English Revolution by the 'middle sort' and bears comparison with the role of the students in the

144 K Lindley, op cit, pp149, 226-229, 253, 300.
145 An Humble Declaration of the Apprentices and other Young Men of the City of London, op cit; The Humble Petition of Many Thousands of Young Men, and Apprentices of the City of London (1647); The Thankfull Acknowledgment and Congratulation of Divers well-affected Apprentices Within the Ward of Cripple-gate without (1649); The Humble Petition of Divers well-affected... Youngmen and Apprentices of the Cities of London and Westminster, Borough of Southwark, and Parts Adjacent (1653); The Remonstrance of the Apprentices in and About London (1659).
146 P Higgins, 'The Reactions of Women, with Special Reference to Women Petitioners', in B Manning (ed), Politics, Religion and the English Civil War, op cit, pp210-222.

revolutions of 1848, who also came from artisan and peasant backgrounds, and 'generally represented the bourgeois middle'.[147]

Restraints on popular revolutionary action

The ruling order was maintained by the economic and political power of the great landlords and big merchants. A contemporary said that the gentry 'can, and indeed have done, and in most cases do still keep the poor in such subjection, that not only their own tenants, but other poor that live near them, must run and go, and work, and obey them as they shall please to command them, else they run the hazard of being undone'.[148] Radicals were well aware that only members of the ruling class were elected to parliament because 'the persons choosing are commonly more swayed by favour than reason in their choice, being tenants either to the persons chosen, or their friends'.[149] People voted for their landlord or a rich man rather 'than hazard his frown, or the lords' and ladies' displeasure who solicited for him'.[150] Lilburne asserted that the electorate in many boroughs consisted of 'ignorant sots, who want principles to choose any man but only those that either some lord or great man writes for and recommends, or else one who bribes them for their votes'.[151]

There was a widespread acceptance that only the nobles and the wealthy were fitted to rule, those who by their upbringing or education or experience were prepared for the job and had the leisure to devote to it, and an extraordinary illusion that they would be less liable than poorer men to be influenced by bribes or particular interests. Peasants and artisans lacked these qualifications.[152] Although George Wither urged the electorate to choose for parliament men 'rather eminent for their virtues and abilities, than for their wealth, birth or titles', he warned against choosing men so poor that their necessities would make them liable to take bribes.[153] Walwyn was accused of finding fault 'that riches and estates, and the things of this world should prefer men to offices and places of trust', and saying 'that virtue, though in poor men, should be more regarded, as in butchers or cobblers'. He replied: 'Who ever heard me speak

147 A Klíma, op cit, p76.
148 W Cole, *A Rod for the Lawyers* (London, 1659), pp7-8.
149 'Sirrahniho' (John Harris), *The Grand Designe* (1647).
150 G Wither, *Letters of Advice Touching the Choice of Knights and Burgesses for the Parliament* (London, 1645), pp5, 20.
151 J Lilburne, *Londons Liberty in Chains Discovered* (1646), p53.
152 G De Ste Croix, op cit, pp411, 413.
153 G Wither, op cit, p8.

either in behalf of butchers or cobblers as to places of government? I profess I know not where, nor when.' He added, however, with characteristic ambiguity, which nevertheless accepted the common prejudice against such an idea: 'But by the way, I am not so strong as to talk usually after this rule, I know the generality of our times cannot bear it'.[154]

The extent of the acceptance of the principle of a hierarchy of rank, wealth and power was reflected in the radicals themselves. The Leveller leaders declared:

> For distinctions of order and dignities, we think them so needful, as they are animosities of virtue, or requisite for the maintenance of the magistracy and government, we think they were never intended for the nourishment of ambition, or subjugation of the people, but only to preserve the due respect and obedience in the people which is necessary for the better execution of the laws.[155]

William Sprigge, who was elected a fellow of Lincoln College at the University of Oxford on Cromwell's recommendation and then became one of the first fellows of Cromwell's new university at Durham, wanted to see 'a more equal and righteous' distribution of wealth and a law putting an upper limit on the amount of land any one person might own: 'Not that I would introduce a levelling of all estates and families to the same proportion, which were absurd and ridiculous', but he thought it necessary to keep up the gentry 'for management of the most important affairs of the nation'.[156] Lilburne assured Lord Wharton that the Levellers would preserve his property in his great estates and his hereditary titles.[157] A very radical pamphlet which fiercely attacked the rich and their oppression of the poor, and expressed great hostility towards the House of Lords and the rulers of the City of London, nevertheless concluded: 'We desire only some competency of means whereby to live quietly, that we be not chargeable, but rather helpful to the commonwealth, and no wise to disturb you, either in your wealth or honours'.[158]

A hierarchical society was preserved by the prospect of rising further up the rungs of wealth, status and power. Yeoman farmers aspired to

154 J R McMichael and B Taft (eds), op cit, pp417-418.
155 D M Wolfe (ed), op cit, p391.
156 W Sprigge, A Modest Plea, For an Equal Common-wealth, Against Monarchy (London, 1659); R L Greaves, 'William Sprigge and the Cromwellian Revolution', The Huntington Library Quarterly, vol XXXIV (1970-71).
157 J Lilburne, An Impeachment of High Treason Against Oliver Cromwel (London, 1649), p41.
158 Englands Troublers Troubled (1648), pp10-11.

become gentry, master craftsmen to be merchant capitalists, journeymen and apprentices to be master craftsmen. The poor had little or no hope of rising and so solaced themselves with fantasies of miraculous transitions from poverty to riches. The popular fable of Thomas Hickathrift, according to Margaret Spufford, 'accurately reflects the aspirations of the rural poor'. He is the son of the widow of a poor labourer. He is physically strong and intellectually weak. He fights and kills a giant, from whose cave he acquires a fortune in gold and silver:

> Tom pulled down the cave, and built him a...house where the cave stood, all the ground that the giant kept by force and strength, some he gave to the poor [to be] their common, and the rest he made pastures of, and divided the most part...to maintain him and his old mother... And Tom's fame was spread both far and near throughout the country, and then it was no longer Tom but Mr Hickathrift, so that he was the chiefest man amongst them... Tom kept men and maids and lived most bravely, and he made him a park to keep deer in and by his house...he built a famous church.[159]

'In fact he behaved as a country gentleman, and, presumably, as the reader would do if he could.' This may well reflect 'the aspirations of the poor' and admiration for the lifestyle of the rich, but for Spufford to say that 'there is no social protest here' and no 'dream of changing their social order' is myopic. While it cannot be known for certain what the audience derived from such a story, the question may be asked, what did the giant symbolise? He had acquired his land and wealth 'by force and strength', just as it was assumed the ruling class had, and he could be overcome only by force and strength. His wealth was redistributed to a poor boy, who further redistributed some of it to other poor people, and it is significant that he gave it in the form of a common at a time when commons were being taken from the poor. He is successful despite his lack of gentle birth, education and intellect—the qualities which according to the ruling culture should have distinguished a 'Mr' and 'the chiefest man amongst them'. It savours of the 'world turned upside down', which involves the poor and humble assuming the attributes of the rich and powerful. The envy of the poor was assuaged by the fact that Tom was bored by his new life. The tale is an acceptance of the realities of the social order, but at the same time it mocks that order by making it accessible to a poor simpleton. It may be questioned how far the poor did accept the culture of their rulers.

159 M Spufford, *Small Books and Pleasant Histories*, op cit, pp248-249.

The popular story of Dick Whittington's rise from poor apprentice to Lord Mayor of London captured the 'combination of miracle and dream fulfilment' with the added reality that Sir Richard Whittington actually was Lord Mayor of London three times in the 15th century. 'Whittington's passage from rags to riches must have been the very stuff of young apprentices' hopes, or at least dreams, reconciling them to the inevitable long years of servitude.' 'In an era in which the moralist never ceased harping on the need to remain without complaint or striving in the status to which one was born and the calling to which one was summoned by god', comments Paul S Seaver, 'the story of Dick Whittington presented an alternative morality played out in the arena...where striving was sanctioned and rising was part of the divine plan.' Success in the commercial and industrial metropolis came from not remaining in one's station:

> And you poor country boys
> Though born of low degree
> See by God's Providence
> What you in time may be.[160]

It was, however, a story which made hierarchy more acceptable by introducing the prospect of upward mobility.

How deep was the deference of the poor towards the rich? A modern historian writes that 'the poor labourer anxious to keep his family fed had to maintain the proper attitude towards his betters: from them came work, credit and poor relief.' But in their hearts how deferential were they? A writer in 1657 described 'labouring poor men which in times of scarcity pine and murmur for want of bread, cursing the rich behind his back, and before his face, cap and knee and a whining countenance'. J A Sharpe comments, 'Contemporaries were aware that the apparent passivity and deference of the poor did not imply an absence of social tension or plebeian discontent: historians would do well to follow this example'.[161] 'Deference...cannot be taken at more than its face value and semblance', writes K D M Snell:

> For that, after all, is all labourers intended of it... Deferential attitudes became a manner, one side of an habitual double faced outlook, a form of self preservation. They were buttoned in as a necessity for survival,

160 P S Seaver, 'Declining Status in an Aspiring Age', op cit, pp129-131; P Burke, 'Popular Culture in Seveteenth-Century London', in B Reay (ed), *Popular Culture in Seventeenth-Century England*, op cit, pp53-54.
161 J A Sharpe, *Early Modern England: A Social History 1550-1760* (London, second edition, 1988), p224.

insisted upon by vulnerable parents from an early age, parents who despaired at gross and often capricious landed power, who felt themselves without the slightest influence to change a seemingly immutable social structure.

But deference often concealed a deep sense of grievance and social bitterness.[162]

But how radical were the people? Lukács's observations are applicable to the English civil war:

> No civil war in history has been so violent as to turn the entire population without exception into fanatical partisans of one or other of the contending camps. Large sections of people have always stood between the camps with fluctuating sympathies now for this side, now for the other. And these fluctuating sympathies have often played a decisive role in the actual outcome of the crisis. In addition, the daily life of the nation still goes on amidst the most terrible civil war...and this continuation of daily life is an important foundation for the continuity of cultural development. Of course, the continuation of daily life certainly does not mean that the life, thought and experience of these non- or not passionately participant popular masses can remain untouched by the historical crisis.[163]

This is illustrated by the popular movement in the west of England towards the end of the civil war known as the 'risings of the clubmen', in which peasants 'clubbed together'—formed associations—to protect their localities against the depredations of the soldiers of both sides and to persuade the king and parliament to make peace. This movement (or more correctly series of movements) has been seized upon by revisionist historians as evidence that during the English Revolution there was greater popular support for conservatism than for radicalism. John Morrill says that 'the radical conservatism of the clubmen was to prove more characteristic of the later 1640s than the iconoclasm of the Levellers'.[164] Dow stresses 'the weakness of the attraction which new visions of society held for the lower classes', and that 'the governed' were more attracted to conservative than to radical views—the traditional monarchical constitution and the traditional Church of England. In a somewhat bizarre structuring of her book she places the clubmen in the same chapter with the Diggers, but her aim is to show that 'the

---

162 K D M Snell, op cit, p165.
163 G Lukács, *The Historical Novel*, translated by H and S Mitchell (London, 1962), p37.
164 J Morrill, *The Revolt of the Provinces: Conservatives and Radicals in the English Civil War 1630-1650* (1976, reprinted London, 1980), p88.

Digger movement was untypical of popular action', the clubmen being far more typical and much closer to the popular mentality.[165] But the dividing line between 'conservative' and 'radical' is fragile: some clubmen attacked enclosures.[166] Jack A Goldstone points out that 'popular reactions are often conservative in tone', appealing to customs and traditions. The risings of the clubmen were movements of local communities defending themselves against destructive pressures from outside. The peasant ideal was 'a village free from outside interference', whether by the parties in the civil war or by enclosing landlords, and could as well mean a village free from the exactions of landlords or the tithes demanded by the clergy.[167]

There is a question then about the meaning and import of describing the masses as 'conservative', but the fact remains that popular support for radical movements was limited and for the ideas of the far left not very evident. The Levellers themselves were not unaware of this. When they were campaigning in January 1648 for support for a petition to the House of Commons, Lilburne and Wildman attended a meeting at Wapping where 'some honest people...scrupled to petition any more to the House'. When Lilburne said that a petition supported by the generality of the people would have some impact, it was objected that 'for anything could be perceived, the generality of the people were as willing to be slaves, as any were to have them so; and having been so often jaded, had sat down with a kind of resolution to stir no more come what would come; therefore we being but a small number to the whole, our striving in this case was but to sow the wind.' 'It was further objected that the people all over the kingdom were generally very ignorant, and malignant [ie royalist], and hated the parliament and us.' Under the parliament their 'oppressions and burdens' had grown greater than before, 'and for all their expenses and fightings were never a bit freer, either at present, or in future grounded hopes.' Lilburne did not attempt to deny this, agreeing that 'the people are generally malignant, and more for the king than the parliament, but what's the reason? But because their burdens are greater now than before.' They are ignorant because parliament told them it fought for their liberties but never spelt out what exactly they were. The function of the petition was to 'beget understanding and knowledge in the people,

165 F D Dow, op cit, pp74, 79, 80, 81-82.
166 B Sharp, *In Contempt of All Authority: Rural Artisans and Riot in the West of England, 1586-1660* (Berkeley, 1980), pp240-242, 248.
167 J A Goldstone, *Revolution and Rebellion in the Early Modern World* (Berkeley, 1991), pp419-420.

when they should hear it, and read it, and discourse upon it; and if nothing but that was effected, our labour would not be totally lost.' What was needed was 'a vigorous proposing and prosecuting of some universal just things to ease them, and for the future to secure them; neither was there any safe or sure way for the people to act in, to make their grievances known and probably hope for redress, but by petition, and that to the House of Commons'.[168] The meeting took place 'at the house of one Williams a gardener' and was attended by 'plain men', thus showing that ordinary people were involved in political debate, even though a 'small number'. The question proved to be the perennial one whether a more radical or a more conservative policy would win popular support.

Class conflict was often expressed through an ideological framework provided by religion. Petegorsky, more than any other historian, considers that it is 'indisputable' that the religion of the far left 'was the product of an acute class consciousness':

> There is vehement denunciation of the rich for their exploitation of the poor; there is fiery condemnation of class oppression. And that protest is inspired...not merely by moral or ethical considerations, but by the recognition that the luxury of the rich is the product of the exploitation and destitution of the poor.[169]

Max Weber analysed the religions of the 'privileged' and the 'non-privileged' classes, and attributed to the lowest and most 'disprivileged' a religion which sought 'reward for one's own good deeds and punishment for the unrighteousness of others', which could be translated into the belief 'that the unequal distribution of mundane goods is caused by the sinfulness and the illegality of the privileged, and that sooner or later god's wrath will overtake them'.[170] The millenarian context of much of radicalism during the English Revolution—that the Second Coming of Jesus Christ would cast down the rich and redeem the poor—provided a revolutionary ideology, but one that was bound to fade, as it did in the 1650s, with the realisation that the millennium was not imminent: it was indeed a god that failed. The notion that divine intervention would change the world confirmed people in their acceptance that to do this was not in their own power,

---

168 J Lilburne, *An Impeachment of High Treason Against Oliver Cromwel*, op cit, pp22-27; J Wildman, *Truths Triumph, or Treachery Anatomized* (London, 1648); W Haller and G Davies (eds), op cit, pp97-104.

169 D W Petegorsky, op cit, pp235-237.

170 M Weber, op cit, pp106-110.

that revolution would not come from themselves but from an outside force.

Religion could justify rejection of the existing social order and indeed sanction rebellion against it, but religion could also justify obedience to the existing social order and sanctify submission to it. The question arises whether religion was a more powerful force for social control or for social protest. Winstanley was clear enough that religion as it was taught to the people by the clergy diverted them from seeking to change the world:

> For while men are gazing up to heaven, imagining after a happiness, or fearing a hell after they are dead, their eyes are put out, and they see not what is their birthright, and what is to be done by them here on earth while they are living.[171]

The general reflections of De Ste Croix are persuasive:

> I doubt if a better means could have been devised of distracting the victims of the class struggle from thinking about their own grievances and possible ways of remedying them than representing to them, as their ecclesiastical leaders did, that religious issues were infinitely more important than social, economic or political ones, and that it was heretics and schismatics…upon whom their resentment could most profitably be concentrated. Of course I am not saying that leading ecclesiastics magnified the importance of theological questions with the deliberate aim of distracting the common herd from their temporal grievances: they themselves quite sincerely held that only adherence to the 'right' dogma and the 'right' sect could ensure salvation and escape from the frightful prospect of eternal damnation.

People were persuaded 'that their real enemies were those enemies of god and his church who, if they were not suppressed, would endanger men's immortal souls and bring them to perdition'.[172] Religion focused popular hostility on 'papists' in 1640-42, thus helping to bring down the government of Charles I, but in 1659-60 religion focused popular hostility on the Quakers, thus helping to bring down the republic.[173] It may have diverted popular anger away from big landlords, whose economic power it thus helped to preserve and whose return to political power it thus helped to facilitate.

---

171 G H Sabine (ed), op cit, p569.
172 G E M De Ste Croix, op cit, p452.
173 B Reay, *The Quakers*, op cit, p100.

It may also be argued that the preoccupation of the Levellers and other radicals with constitutional issues diverted efforts from attacking the more fundamental issues of the economic and social power of landlords. That is what William Sprigge put forward in his pamphlet *A Modest Plea, For an Equal Common-wealth, Against Monarchy*, which appeared in two editions during the critical discussions of the constitution of the republic in 1659, and, according to his friend Anthony Wood, was 'greedily bought up, and taken into the hands of all curious men' and highly commended. He said that he did not give a 'bullrush' whether there was a House of Lords or some other form of second chamber, or whether there was an annual parliament or an everlasting parliament, for either way nothing would change so long as the legislature was dominated by big landlords:

> Is this suitable to a commonwealth? Or was this the design of our Reformation, to put the whole land into the hands of a few proprietors? Was it for this end abbeys were demolished, and the hierarchy taken down, that a few gentlemen...might have their lands, because they had not enough before? Is this the purchase of all our blood and treasure to set up a few more great families, to increase the number of our masters?... What then will become of our Free State? Will not our landlords erect what government they please over us?[174]

The far left visualised a far reaching revolution, breaking totally with the past, as the author of *Tyranipocrit* said:

> It is not new forms, but a new condition that we do want, we have no need of tyranny in a new fashion, but of a changing of manners and customs, which are evil and prejudicial to the commonwealth, into such as may be beneficial to all mankind.[175]

This revolution was to be made by those Winstanley called 'the poor' and 'the lowest and despised sort of people'.[176] But the emerging proletariat to which the far left appealed was described by Eduard Bernstein, who pioneered the history of the far left in the English Revolution, as 'an inchoate class'.[177] That judgement is supported by the evidence in chapter one on the varying degrees of independence and dependence amongst artisans, on the fact that many wage earners did

---

174 W Sprigge, op cit; R L Greaves, op cit.
175 *Tyranipocrit*, op cit, p36.
176 G H Sabine (ed), op cit, pp186, 205.
177 E Bernstein, op cit, pp131, 170; F Engels, *The Peasant War in Germany*, op cit, pp115-116.

not depend wholly on wages for their livelihoods, and on the overlap between small peasants and labourers, as well as the uncertain and shifting boundaries between 'the middle sort' and 'the poor'.

Chapter 3

Revolt

The previous chapter considered 'moral force' radicalism, which sought to achieve its objectives by the persuasion of manifestos and symbolic acts, and ruled out the use of physical force. This chapter will examine 'physical force' radicalism, which aimed to overthrow the regime by armed revolt: firstly, the Leveller revolt led by William Thompson in 1649, and secondly the Fifth Monarchist revolt led by Thomas Venner in 1657. These were small events in themselves, and since the first was rapidly crushed and the second never got off the ground, they may appear insignificant. But both were connected with, and arose out of the main radical movements of the period—the Levellers and the Fifth Monarchists—and the question of whether or not to resort to force against the government of the Commonwealth (1649-53) or the Protectorate (1653-59) exercised the minds of Levellers and Fifth Monarchists and radicals in general (the Quakers had not yet become pacifists). Further than that the whole question of violent revolution is involved.

The English Revolution began in violence with a bloody civil war and was consummated by a military *coup d'état* in 1648. The government of Charles I did not have a standing army and was at the mercy of the crowds which demonstrated in London in 1640-42. The governments of the Commonwealth and Protectorate did have a standing army. A lesson which Marx derived from the revolutions of 1848-49 was that 're-bellion in the old style, street fighting with barricades, which decided the issue everywhere up to 1848, was to a considerable extent obso-lete'.[1] Lenin concluded in 1906: 'And now we must at last openly and publicly admit that political strikes are inadequate; we must carry on the widest agitation among the masses in favour of an armed uprising... It is alleged that it is impossible to fight modern troops; the troops must become revolutionary. Of course, unless the revolution assumes a mass

---

1   K Marx, 'The Class Struggles in France 1848 to 1850', in K Marx and F Engels, *Selected Works*, vol I (2 vols, Moscow, 1949-50), p120.

character and also affects the troops, serious fighting is out of the question.' This, he recognised, was not a new factor in revolution: 'not a single great revolution has ever taken place, or ever will take place, without the "disorganisation" of the army'.[2] 'There is no doubt', wrote Trotsky, 'that the fate of every revolution at a certain point is decided by a break in the disposition of the army. Against a numerous, disciplined, well-armed and ably led military force, unarmed or almost unarmed masses of the people cannot possibly gain a victory'.[3]

The Levellers in the English Revolution in fact pursued a dual policy of seeking to win the soldiers over to their cause and of organising a mass popular movement by petitions and demonstrations. While Thompson in the first place looked to inciting the soldiers to mutiny and Venner to armed civilians overcoming the soldiers, both hoped to arouse mass popular support. 'Moral force' and 'physical force' were not at opposite poles but close to each other, and armed uprising and peaceful demonstration were compatible tactics. Indeed, without a mass popular movement there would not be 'a break in the disposition of the army' and without 'a break in the disposition of the army' the mass popular movement could not succeed. Neither condition was met in the unsuccessful revolts of Thompson and Venner. Historians tend to be too preoccupied with successful movements, but unsuccessful movements are as much a part of history, and in the present cases may inform us about both the weaknesses of radicalism and the nature of the English Revolution.

The Corporal's Revolt, 1649

In 1647 William Thompson was corporal of Captain Pitchford's troop in Colonel Whalley's regiment of horse. He first came to notice as a result of a tavern brawl, about which an inordinate amount has been written then and since, but suffice it to say that he confessed his fault and never denied that it arose from 'my extreme folly, which I do not so much as in a thought justify.' 'I desire', he pleaded, 'my life may not be measured by one simple action'. Nevertheless his life has been so measured by his contemporaries and by modern historians. For this offence he was dismissed from the army, which he thought was a punishment

2   V I Lenin, 'The Lessons of the Moscow Uprising' (1906) in V I Lenin, *Selected Works*, vol I (2 vols, London, 1947), p446, and 'The Proletarian Revolution and the Renegade Kautsky' (1918), in V I Lenin, *Selected Works*, vol II (2 vols, London, 1947), p402.
3   L Trotsky, *The History of the Russian Revolution*, translated by M Eastman (1932-33, reprinted London, 1977), pp139-141.

disproportionate to the crime, and he suspected that the officers found in the affair a pretext to rid themselves of a trouble making radical, a suspicion shared by H N Brailsford and Christopher Hill. He received some sympathy and support from fellow soldiers in the troop.[4]

From now on he associated himself with the Levellers and particularly with John Lilburne. It was alleged that his radicalism sprang from resentment at the way in which he had been treated by the officers, and 'to revenge himself, sought to make division in the army, and by his seditious and traitorous practices, became a chief man and a ringleader among the Levellers'.[5] But he was probably a radical before this, for he belonged to the most radical troop in one of the most radical regiments in the army. The moderate puritan minister, Richard Baxter, was shocked by the influence of the radical religious sects on some of the soldiers, especially in Whalley's regiment, of which he was briefly chaplain after the battle of Naseby (1645), and he singled out Captain Pitchford's troop as the most heretical:

> They...most vehemently declaimed against the doctrine of Election, and for the power of Free Will... And they cried down all our ministry, Episcopal, Presbyterian and Independent; and all our churches... They were vehement against the king, and all government but popular; and against magistrates meddling in matters of religion... These were the same men that afterward were called Levellers.[6]

Christopher Hill has shown that rejection of 'the doctrine of Election'—the Calvinist dogma of predestination by which god had decreed from the beginning who would be saved and who would be damned (the assumption being that only a few would go to heaven and most would go to hell)—and the belief that all had free will and could save themselves, often marked off the more radical from the more moderate revolutionaries. And Murray Tolmie has demonstrated that the Levellers were associated especially with the General Baptists, who repudiated the elitist doctrine of predestination (in contrast to the Calvinistic Particular Baptists), and with those religious radicals who believed in the democratic doctrine of universal redemption, that all would be saved. The General Baptists derived much of their strength from the small tradesmen and artisans of London, and they

---

4   W Thompson, *A True and Impartial Relation* (1648), pp1-5, 10-11; *A Vindication of Lieut Gen Cromwell, and Com Gen Ireton* (London, 1648); H N Brailsford, *The Levellers and the English Revolution* (London, 1961), p522 n4; C Hill, *The World Turned Upside Down* (London, 1972), p55 n52.
5   *The Discoverer*, part ii (London, 1649), p7.
6   M Sylvester (ed), *Reliquiae Baxterianae* (London, 1696), pp53-54.

were numerous in the lower ranks of Colonel Whalley's regiment and in Captain Pitchford's troop.[7] This was the intellectual milieu from which Corporal Thompson came and in which he learned his radicalism. Also in his troop was Robert Lockyer, who was destined, like Thompson, to become a martyr for the Leveller cause in 1649. Baxter, however, noted that there were others in this troop whose opinions, in his view, were 'much worse' than Thompson's.

The first part of the story of Thompson illustrates the tactic of individual resistance to the power of 'unjust' or 'illegal' authority, and the symbolic gestures of defiance through which class antagonism and revolutionary mentality expressed themselves in 17th century England.

At the time of the Leveller mutinies in the army in November 1647, culminating and collapsing at Corkbush Field, near Ware in Hertfordshire, Thompson (now a civilian) was sent by the Levellers to Suffolk to promote the *Agreement of the People* (their proposed new constitution for England) amongst the men of Colonel Fleetwood's regiment, and to get them to join the revolt. In this he had no success and so went to his old regiment, where he was arrested and imprisoned at Windsor. He was brought before a court martial but denied that it had any jurisdiction over him because he was no longer a soldier. His case was referred to General Fairfax, the commander in chief of the army, and meanwhile Lieutenant-General Cromwell let him out on parole to go to London for a few days about his own affairs (which no doubt included contact with Lilburne). It is characteristic of Thompson that he was punctilious about keeping his word of honour: he duly returned from his parole and rendered himself a prisoner again. Then he escaped, leaving a letter for Fairfax, 'in which I gave his excellency to understand therein, that I acknowledge in them no jurisdiction over me':

> Therefore, I cannot in the least give you any honour, reverence or respect, either in word, action, or gesture; and if you by force and compulsion compel me again to come before you, I must and will by god's assistance keep on my hat, and look upon you as a company of murderers, robbers and thieves, and do the best I can to raise the hue and cry of the kingdom against you.[8]

7   C Hill, *Milton and the English Revolution* (1977, reprinted London, 1997), ch 21;
     M Tolmie, *The Triumph of the Saints: The Separate Churches of London 1616-49*
     (Cambridge, 1977), pp69-74, 151-154, 157-158; J F McGregor, 'The Baptists: Fount of
     All Heresy', in J F McGregor and B Reay, *Radical Religion in the English Revolution*
     (Oxford, 1984); A Laurence, *Parliamentary Army Chaplains 1642-1651*, Royal Historical
     Society Studies in History 59 (1990), p84; *Tyranipocrit* (Rotterdam, 1649), pp11-12.
8   D M Wolfe (ed), *Leveller Manifestoes of the Puritan Revolution* (1944, reprinted London,
     1967), pp242-258; W Thompson, *A True and Impartial Relation*, op cit, pp5-7;

'A company of murderers': the reference was to the shooting to death of Private Richard Arnold at the head of his regiment on Corkbush Field after a drumhead court martial for mutiny. The rejection of the requirement to doff one's hat before superiors was a traditional act of refusal to accept their authority, regularly used by Lilburne. Thompson published his letter to Fairfax as a pamphlet, taking its title from the slogan of the Leveller mutineers at Corkbush Field, *England's Freedom, Soldiers' Rights*, which was a contribution to a continuing Leveller campaign that martial law was illegal in time of peace and that trials should be before juries in the ordinary courts. Modern historians generally think that it was written by Lilburne.[9]

In February 1648, according to Thompson's own account, he was 'about my lawful occasions at the House of Commons' door, to speak with a member of the said House', but according to the army authorities he was 'endeavouring to stir up mutinous distempers' amongst the soldiers stationed at Westminster. At this time the Levellers were renewing their propaganda amongst the private soldiers, and one of their most class conscious manifestos, *The Mournfull Cries of Many Thousand Poor Tradesmen*, included a specific appeal to the soldiers to sign the Levellers' petition of 19 January and to demonstrate their support for it at the doors of parliament. Lazarus Tindall, a private soldier in Colonel Barkstead's regiment, was given copies to distribute amongst his comrades. This regiment was stationed at Whitehall with orders to guard parliament and to prevent Leveller demonstrations, and so campaigning by the Levellers amongst the men of this regiment was certain to cause the maximum alarm in the high command. When Lieutenant-General Cromwell and Commissary-General Ireton came out of the House of Commons they spotted Thompson, arrested him and handed him over to a court martial. Bills were posted up in London protesting that trial by a military court was a violation of the rights of a free commoner (a title in which Thompson delighted), and a threat to the 'estates, liberties, and lives of all the free commons of England'.

At the court martial, which was presided over by Fairfax, Thompson exhibited a mixture of social deference with a capacity for dramatising

A *Vindication of Lieut Gen Cromwell, and Com Gen Ireton*, op cit, pp3-4; *The Iustice of the Army Against Evill-Doers Vindicated* (London, 1649), pp7-9.

9   T C Pease, *The Leveller Movement* (1916, reprinted Gloucester, Mass, 1965), p230; H N Brailsford, op cit, p299; A Woolrych, *Soldiers and Statesmen: The General Council of the Army and its Debates, 1647-1648* (Oxford, 1987), p293; I Gentles, *The New Model Army in England, Ireland and Scotland, 1645-53* (Oxford, 1992), pp316-317.

his case for popular consumption by symbolic acts of non-violent resistance, modelling himself on Lilburne's defiance of the Court of Star Chamber in 1638 and of the House of Lords in 1646:

> I demeaned myself with all civility and respect, as they were gentlemen, but withal declared, that I could not in the least submit to them, as a court having power to take cognisance of any real or supposed crime that could be laid to my charge, I being by their own votes no member of the army; but I declared, that if they had anything to lay to my charge, the ordinary courts of justice were all open and free, where I should be ready to answer what could be legally objected against me.

All this while he had stood respectfully bareheaded. Cromwell sneered that he had not been as good as his word to keep his hat on in the presence of Fairfax. At this Thompson clapped his hat on his head and made to leave. He was forcibly restrained and his hat knocked from his head. 'After which I manifested myself more resolvedly, declaring them to be actual destroyers of the laws and liberties of England, and so were become the greatest apostates in the world...upon which I threw Magna Carta and the Petition of Right upon the table before them' (a characteristically Lilburnian gesture).

Thompson was taken out and held in another room, where he reflected, 'I was merely in their hands because they were stronger than I', and so recognising passive resistance as the only weapon of the weak against the strong, when summoned back before the court, 'I resolved to manifest my integrity to my native country's freedom by being merely passive in their hands.' He refused to walk and had to be carried into the court, where he lay on the floor, and when they asked him questions he stuffed his fingers into his ears so as not to hear them, and when they dragged him to his feet and pulled his hands from his head, he talked loudly and continuously so as to drown their voices. He was found guilty of attaching himself to the army and pretending to be a soldier, though not listed in any troop or company; of inciting the soldiers to seditious uproar; and of denying the jurisdiction of the court. He was sentenced to death, but with the 'privilege' of being shot rather than hanged. 'His unparalleled insolent, contemptuous, contumelious, and menacing carriage against the General and the whole council at his trial' was deemed not becoming 'a Christian or a civil man'. Fairfax, however, reprieved him from death, but kept him in prison. Lilburne took up and supported his case in two pamphlets. With the outbreak of the Second Civil War in 1648 and the departure of the army from London, Thompson escaped from prison, or perhaps he was released, for at this time the chief officers and the radicals were reconciled in face of the common enemy.[10]

Thompson reappears in March 1649, entitling himself a captain with a band of armed men that he called his troop. He was arrested for attacking a gentleman's house in Essex. Barbara Taft says that he had become an outlaw at the head of a gang of robbers, and Brailsford suggested that he was playing the part of a Robin Hood. It is tempting to equate him with Eric Hobsbawm's social bandits but there is no evidence to support the views of Taft and Brailsford. It is more likely that during the Second Civil War, like many radicals, he raised a force to fight the royalists. For example, Henry Marten raised in Berkshire a regiment allegedly composed of Levellers under the slogan 'freedom and common justice against tyranny and oppression'. He took upon himself to appoint officers 'by virtue of that right which I was born to as an Englishman and in pursuance of that duty which I owe my said country'. Although he was accused of being 'all for parity and anarchy', he issued a declaration denying any intention of levelling property. In the summer and autumn of 1648 there was emerging a radical army alongside the regular army, but early in 1649 Fairfax was busy disbanding these irregular or supernumerary units which had been mobilised to fight the Second Civil War. Thompson claimed to have a commission to raise a troop but Fairfax denied this, and the clash in Essex seems to have arisen from Thompson seeking to billet at free-quarter his unpaid irregular force. He was taken to the army's headquarters at Whitehall but it was found that he was not a soldier—necessarily so because otherwise it would have substantiated his defence—and he was handed over to a civil magistrate in Essex, who bound him over for trial at the assizes. Significantly, it was the Leveller leaders John Lilburne and John Harris who stood bail for him, showing his continuing close links with the Leveller leadership.[11]

10   D M Wolfe (ed), op cit, pp277-278; W Haller and G Davies (eds), *The Leveller Tracts 1647-1653* (1944, reprinted Gloucester, Mass, 1964), pp101, 125-126; C H Firth and G Davies, *The Regimental History of Cromwell's Army*, vol I (2 vols, Oxford, 1940), p339; W Thompson, *A True and Impartial Relation*, op cit, pp8-11; *A Vindication of Lieut Gen Cromwell, and Com Gen Ireton*, op cit, pp5-6; *The Iustice of the Army Against Evill-Doers Vindicated*, op cit, p9; *The Prisoners Plea for a Habeas Corpus* (1648); J Lilburne, *The Prisoners Mournfull Cry* (1648).

11   *Perfect Occurrences* (2-9 March 1649); *The Impartiall Intelligencer* (7-14 March 1649); C H Firth (ed), 'The Clarke Papers', vol II, *Camden Society*, new series, vol LIV (1894), pp199-200; *The Iustice of the Army Against Evill-Doers Vindicated*, op cit, p9; *The Discoverer*, part ii, p19; B Taft's entry for W Thompson in R Greaves and R Zaller (eds), *Biographical Dictionary of British Radicals in the Seventeenth Century* (3 vols, Brighton, 1982-84); H N Brailsford, op cit, p522 n4; E J Hobsbawm, *Bandits* (London, 1969); S Barber, ' "A Bastard Kind of Militia": Localism and Tactics in the Second Civil War', in I Gentles, J Morrill and B Worden (eds), *Soldiers, Writers and Statesmen of the English Revolution* (Cambridge, 1998) pp138-139, 141-142.

'He no sooner had his liberty', said the army authorities, 'but without cause or provocation, stabbed one Mr Hayden with a dagger, of which wounds he is since dead.' But Hayden was probably a government agent searching for unlicensed pamphlets—perhaps Lilburne's *The Second Part of England's New-Chaines Discove*red or the anonymous *The English Souldiers Standard*, for both of which the Council of State had ordered searches to be made and their authors, printers and publishers to be arrested and prosecuted. It is likely that Thompson was defending an underground press.[12]

The next part of the story of William Thompson raises the question of the relationship between 'moral force' and 'physical force' in Leveller thinking. There is a consensus amongst historians that the Levellers did not believe in achieving their aims by force. 'There can be no doubt whatever that in spite of the call of Lilburne and Overton in 1647 for the people to rise, and in spite of the mutinies of Leveller soldiers in the army', writes Perez Zagorin, 'the Levellers did not regard force as a normal or a desirable method of effecting political change.' 'One method which, on the whole, the Levellers did not espouse was the use of organised violence or armed rebellion', says F D Dow:

> Few contemplated the violent overthrow of the regime by an armed citizenry, or even by the New Model Army. Of course, the Levellers sought to influence the army, and radical supporters in the rank and file provoked mutinies...but this did not amount to an overall plan for the armed takeover of the regime.

A S P Woodhouse argued that when they appeared to countenance the use of force, it was an aberration:

> They...were passionately devoted to the democratic ideal: taking justice and equality as the foundation of their scheme; believing in truth and agreement through free discussion; in their hearts distrusting force even as a method of effecting beneficient ends and even when betrayed into acquiescing in its use; willing, when truest to themselves, to postpone victory till reason, and not the sword, could win it...

Morrill and Walter conclude that the Levellers:

---

12 *The Iustice of the Army Against Evill-Doers Vindicated*, op cit, p9; *The Discoverer*, part ii, op cit, p19: *The Same Hand Again* (London, 1649); H N Brailsford, op cit, p522 n4; *Commons Journals*, vol VI (1648-51), p175; *Calendar of State Papers Domestic 1649-1650*, pp55, 56, 59, 67, 528.

never appear to have contemplated raising their supporters in armed insurrections... There was certainly a rhetoric of violence at times, but the principal thrust of all the leaders...was to emphasise moral force rather than physical force. They believed in the self evident justice of their cause, and assumed that it would capture the hearts and minds of all whose attention could be attracted. There was a potentiality for violence in Leveller determination, but it was never realised.

There is a disposition amongst these historians to portray the Levellers as non-violent liberal democrats and to gloss over evidence to the contrary. But Christopher Hill detects a physical force wing to the movement, which was perhaps politically and socially more radical than the 'moderate, constitutional wing'.[13]

E P Thompson pointed out, in relation to early 19th century English radicalism, that it is a mistake to make too sharp a distinction between moral force and physical force:

> Few reformers before 1839 engaged in serious preparations for insurrection; but fewer still were willing to disavow altogether the ultimate right of the people to resort to rebellion in the face of tyranny. The Chartist slogan, 'Peaceably if we may, forcibly if we must', expresses also the common notion held by the radicals in 1816-20 and 1830-32.

'Every popular radical journal and orator made some reference, oblique or direct, to the right of rebellion.' But physical force was to be used only when other means—petitioning and demonstrating—failed. John Baxter questions the traditional division of the Chartists 'into moral and physical force factions with the implication that the former adhered to moderate, "legal" or "constitutionalist" action and the latter comprised a small knot of "violent men" committing "extreme", "illegal", "unconstitutional" and "terrorist" acts'. He criticises the histories which ignore or treat as irrelevant the calls to arms, and denigrate them as the 'blustery rhetoric of a few unbalanced or mentally unstable demagogues'. Chartists generally claimed the right of free born Englishmen to take arms to resist a tyrannical government. Charles, Louise and Richard Tilly conclude in their study of collective action in Europe from 1830 to 1930 that there was not 'a sharp

---

13 P Zagorin, *A History of Political Thought in the English Revolution* (1954, reprinted Bristol, 1997), pp40-41; F D Dow, *Radicalism in the English Revolution 1640-1660* (Oxford, 1985), p50; A S P Woodhouse (ed), *Puritanism and Liberty: Being the Army Debates (1647-9)* (London, 1938), Introduction, p98; J Morrill and J Walter, 'Order and Disorder in the English Revolution', in A Fletcher and J Stevenson (eds), *Order and Disorder in Early Modern England* (London, 1985), p161; C Hill, *The World Turned Upside Down*, op cit, pp91-99.

division between violent and non-violent collective action', but rather 'a close connection'. The distinction lay in whether or not the collective action would be more or less likely to lead to violence. Violence was the continuation of previously non-violent campaigning.[14] These analyses are applicable to the Levellers.

The principal interest of Corporal Thompson rests on the fact that he emphasised and implemented physical force Levellerism, and the question is how far this was an aberration or deviation from the mainstream of the movement. When Thompson advocated armed revolt in 1649 he repeated exactly the arguments which the Leveller leader, Richard Overton, had proclaimed in 1647 in his famous manifesto, *An Appeale from Parliament to the People*. Overton held that by the Law of Nature men may defend and deliver themselves 'from all oppression, violence and cruelty whatsoever', and Thompson declared that 'wherefore through an unavoidable necessity, no other means left under heaven, we are enforced to betake ourselves to the Law of Nature, to defend and preserve ourselves and native rights'. When Thompson took to arms he acted on Overton's principle that any individual or private citizen had the right, 'in duty to our own natures, and to our native country in general', to 'rise up, and appear in the defensive cause of this kingdom, for the recovery of our natural human rights and freedom'. Parliament derives its power from the people, and exercises its trust for their good; if it betrays that trust and acts against the safety or freedom of the people, said Overton, power reverts to the people, who:

> by virtue of its instincted, inherent natural sovereignty, may create, or depute any person or persons for their deputy or deputies for the removal of those dead, corrupt, putrefied members from the seat and name of their formal authority, and for suppression of injustice and tyranny, recovery of liberty and freedom. But it may be…that by reason of distraction, confusion and disorder at such an exigency…such a new deputation is not likely, or cannot possibly be formally effected…and therefore by the foresaid permanent unalterable rule of necessity and safety, any person or persons (in discharge of their duty to god, themselves and their country) may warrantably rise up in the cause and behalf of the people, to preserve them from imminent ruin and destruction, such

14   E P Thompson, *The Making of the English Working Class* (Penguin edition, 1968), pp683-685; J Baxter, *Armed Resistance and Insurrection: The Early Chartist Experience*, 'Our History', pamphlet 76 (1984), pp4-8; J Charlton, *The Chartists: The First National Workers' Movement* (A Socialist History of Britain series, London, 1997), pp69-73; C Tilly, L Tilly and R Tilly, *The Rebellious Century 1830-1930* (London, 1975), p282.

person or persons doing in that act no more than every man by nature is bound to perform.[15]

In 1647, in response to its rejection of the radical programme, Lilburne declared that parliament had become:

a conspiracy and confederacy of lawless, unlimited, and unbounded men, that have actually destroyed the laws and liberties of England, and that will have no rule to walk by but their own corrupted and bloody wills, and thereby have set up the highest tyranny that can be set up in the world, against which, by your own principles, the kingdom may justly rise up in arms as one man, and destroy all the aforesaid conspirators without mercy or compassion.[16]

During March and April 1649 there appears to have been a strong current of physical force radicalism running in the Leveller movement and carrying Lilburne and Overton along.[17] Radicals were disappointed that the execution of the king, the abolition of the monarchy and the House of Lords, and the establishment of a republic had not led to the reduction of taxes, the abolition of tithes, the reform of the legal system, and the improvement of the conditions of the poor. The fear on the left was that a military dictatorship was being set up in England. On 28 March the Leveller leaders—John Lilburne, Richard Overton, William Walwyn and Thomas Prince—were arrested and imprisoned in the Tower of London. The Buckinghamshire Levellers called upon the soldiers and all the people of England to resist 'arbitrary powers erected anew' and 'to oppose all tyranny whatsoever, and by whomsoever, intended against us'.[18] Lilburne demanded:

Can those gentlemen sitting at Westminster in the House called the House of Commons, be any other than a factious company of men traitorously combined together with Cromwell, Ireton, and Harrison, to subdue the laws, liberties, and freedom of England...and to set up an absolute and perfect tyranny of the sword, will and pleasure...

Whether the free people of England, as well soldiers as others, ought not to contemn all these men's commands, as invalid and illegal in themselves, and as one man to rise up against them as so many professed traitors, thieves, robbers and highwaymen, and apprehend and bring

15   D M Wolfe (ed), op cit, pp159-162, 173, 176, 178-179, 182, 186; W Thompson, England's Standard Advanced (1649).
16   Quoted in J Frank, The Levellers (Cambridge, Mass, 1955), p121.
17   D M Wolfe (ed), op cit, pp355-382; W Haller and G Davies (eds), op cit, pp171-189.
18   G H Sabine (ed), The Works of Gerrard Winstanley (1941, reprinted New York, 1965), pp637-639.

them to justice in a new Representative [ie parliament], chosen by virtue of a just Agreement among the People, there being no other way in the world to preserve the nation but that alone.[19]

A handbill was distributed in the streets of London on 25 April 1649. It was published simultaneously in the radical newspaper *Mercurius Militaris*, which was edited by the printer and one-time actor John Harris, a leading Leveller and close associate of Lilburne, also linked with Thompson, for whom he had stood bail. Harris may have been the author of this handbill, or conceivably Thompson:

> All worthy officers and soldiers who are yet mindful that you engaged not, as a mere mercenary army, hired to serve the arbitrary ends of a Council of State, but took up arms in judgement and conscience, in behalf of your own and the people's just rights and liberties. You may now see plainly…that the design of our grand officers is…to establish their own absolute power over the commonwealth… And therefore all those officers and soldiers, and all people in all places, are concerned in a very high nature, even as much as the freedom of the nation is worth…to venture their lives, and all they have, to make opposition against this…the greatest treason that ever was committed against the liberties of the people, and not to stand any longer looking on in mizimazi [mizmaze = confusion], betwixt hope and fear, for if this design take place, your great officers and their confederates in parliament and Council of State, will be as so many kings, princes, and lords, and yourselves and all the people their slaves and vassals.[20]

On 1 May 1649 Colonel Scroope's regiment of horse mutinied at Salisbury against the terms offered to those regiments which had been chosen by lot to form the expeditionary force to reconquer Ireland. They were presented with the alternative of receiving two months of their arrears of pay if they agreed to go to Ireland or being cashiered with two weeks pay if they refused. They were joined from Sussex on 11 May by four troops of Commissary-General Ireton's regiment of horse and later by two troops of Colonel Harrison's regiment of horse. This event has become known to history as the 'Burford Mutiny', taking its name from the place where it ended rather than where it began. They directed their appeals for support to the army rather than

---

19 W Haller and G Davies (eds), op cit, pp205-207.
20 A single sheet, printed on one side, without title, British Library E.551(21), and reprinted in *Mercurius Militaris* (17-24 April 1649).

to the people, because their grievance was a military one.[21]

At this time the cavalry regiment of Colonel Reynolds was strung out across the Midlands, with its headquarters at Banbury in Oxfordshire. It had been raised in Kent in 1648 as an additional force to combat the resurgence of royalism in the Second Civil War. It recruited many radicals, some being ex-soldiers who had left the army at the end of 1647, disillusioned by the crushing of the Leveller mutiny at Corkbush Field, and by 'said apprehension of the power of a prevailing party' in the army and 'all the counsels of the nation'. There was strong support for the Levellers in Kent, especially in the Weald, a region of cloth and iron industries, few gentry and many poor people, and a long history of radicalism. The Kent County Committee had complained in March 1649 that many men in this regiment were disaffected to the present government. Captain Bray's troop, which was heavily under Leveller influence, mutinied in the same month. This regiment was not disbanded, however, with the other supernumerary forces, but was assigned to the Irish expedition. It was ordered to march to Anglesey for embarkation, but on 27 April the Council of State wrote to Colonel Reynolds:

> We are weekly informed of the disorders of some of your troopers, who are still very great burdens to the country where they lie, and swear they will not go to Ireland, but rail at the parliament, and show much disaffection to it, and lie in and about Warwickshire, notwithstanding our express orders that they should march into Anglesey.[22]

On 1 May the four Leveller leaders in the Tower published their third and final version of their proposed new constitution for England, *An Agreement of the Free People of England*. About the same time Thompson and some companions went from London to Oxfordshire and Northamptonshire and began to distribute manifestos. Three of them were arrested at Towcester and by order of the Council of State committed to Northampton gaol for spreading 'seditious papers' 'whereby the common people are in danger to be seduced from their

---

21 *The Resolutions of the Private Souldiers of Col Scroops Regiment of Horse* (Salisbury, 1649); *The Unanimous Declaration of Colonel Scroope's, and Commissary Gen Ireton's Regiments* (1649). I Gentles, op cit, p534 n90, is wrong in saying that only three troops of Ireton's regiment joined Scroope's men.

22 J Naylier, *The New Made Colonel or Irelands Jugling Reliever* (London, 1649), pp4-5; J Naylier and J Marshall, *The Foxes Craft Discovered* (1649), p5; P Clark, *English Provincial Society from the Reformation to the Revolution: Politics and Society in Kent 1500-1640* (Hassocks, 1977), p393; C Hill, 'From Lollards to Levellers', in M Cornforth (ed), *Rebels and their Causes: Essays in Honour of A L Morton* (London, 1978), pp51-52; *Calendar of State Papers Domestic 1649-1650*, pp63-64, 66, 68, 94, 98, 111, 125.

duty, and the government undermined'. One of them was named as Valentine Stevens, who may have been the same man as the Valentine Stephenson who had been involved in the mutiny of Bray's troop in Reynolds' regiment in March. On 5 May the Council of State again wrote to Reynolds:

> We hear that divers persons formerly of your regiment have spread dangerous papers in Northamptonshire, tending to the raising of sedition and the destroying of all authority, and boast of having many of your regiment in their party.[23]

On 6 May Thompson launched his insurrection at Banbury, where a rally adopted and proclaimed his manifesto *Englands Standard Advanced*:

> The power of the sword advanced and set in the seat of the magistrates…leaving no visible authority, devolving all into a factious junta and Council of State, usurping and assuming the name, stamp and authority of parliament, to oppress, torment and vex the people, whereby all their lives, liberties, and estates, are all subdued to the wills of those men, no law, no justice, no right or freedom, no ease of grievances, no removal of unjust barbarous taxes, no regard to the cries and groans of the poor to be had while utter beggary and famine (like a mighty torrent) hath broke in upon us, and already seized upon several parts of the nation.
>
> We are gathered and associated together upon the bare account of Englishmen, with our swords in our hands, to redeem ourselves and the land of our nativity from slavery and oppression…to have justice for the blood of M Arnold shot to death at Ware, and for the blood of M Robert Lockyer, and divers others who of late by martial law were murdered at London.
>
> We will endeavour the absolute settlement of this distracted nation upon the form and method by way of an Agreement of the People, tendered as a peace offering by Lieut Col John Lilburne, M Will Walwyn, M Thomas Prince, and M Richard Overton, bearing date 1 May 1649, the which we have annexed to this our Declaration as the standard of our engagement, thereby owning every part and particular of the premises of the said Agreement, promising and resolving to the utmost hazard of our lives and abilities to pursue the speedy and full accomplishment thereof.

They would secure the release of the Leveller leaders 'from their barbarous and illegal imprisonments', and:

---

23   *Calendar of State Papers Domestic 1649-1650*, pp124-126, 531.

protect all to our power from violence and oppression in all places where we come, resolving to stop the payment of all taxes or assessments whatsoever, as of excise, tithes, and the tax of ninety thousand pounds *per mensem*, etc. And having once obtained a new Representative [ie parliament], according to the said Agreement, upon such terms and limitations therein expressed, we shall then freely lay down our arms and return to our several habitations and callings.

This Declaration was designed to be folded and worn in the hat to exhibit the slogan:

FOR A NEW PARLIAMENT,
BY THE AGREEMENT OF THE PEOPLE

'Their professions are very plausible', commented a newspaper, 'as the easing of the people by the taking off taxes and free-quarter.' Some accounts in the press must have generated alarm in the richer classes, embroidering the manifesto with matter not to be found in the text, that it was 'against all government, but by the common people, and some of them have said...that they will have a new parliament in which none shall be chosen that have any estates, but all of the poorer sort; and that thereby they may have poor people in all parts made magistrates'.[24]

'It is a summons rather to rebellion than to mutiny', observed Brailsford. It called upon 'all...to rise up and come in to help a distressed miserable nation to break the bands of cruelty, tyranny, and oppression, and set the people free'. Unlike the Salisbury mutineers, Thompson was not merely inciting soldiers to mutiny. He was calling for a general uprising of the population at large against the government, parliament and high command of the army. But it needs to be stressed that he saw his action as defensive resistance, with the limited objective of securing a new constitution, not as seizing power and ruling the country.[25]

Some degree of advanced planning and preparation had to have been involved, if only to the extent of writing and printing the manifesto and recruiting a small cadre to distribute it. Austin Woolrych says that the manifesto 'has a Lilburnian ring to it'; A L Morton suggested that perhaps it was written by Lilburne; Brailsford thought that 'much of it reads like the work of Freeborn John'; and Barbara Taft judges

24 W Thompson, *Englands Standard Advanced* (2 editions in 1649); *The Impartiall Intelligencer* (2-9 May 1649); *The Kingdomes Weekly Intelligencer* (8-15 May 1649).
25 H N Brailsford, op cit, p513; B Denton, *William Thompson: Leveller, Revolutionary or Mutineer?* (Partizan Press, 1988), pp16, 23-24.

that 'it is unlikely that Thompson' wrote it 'without considerable help—probably from Lilburne'.[26] But it is unsafe to assume that Thompson could not have written it. All contemporary accounts show him to have been articulate and eloquent in speech, he was literate, and many ordinary soldiers in the New Model Army preached sermons and wrote pamphlets. If, however, Lilburne did assist in the composition of Thompson's manifesto then he was implicated in preparing and approving the rising, although it must be stressed that there is no direct evidence for this.

Two troops of Reynolds' regiment rallied to Thompson. So did the Oxfordshire county troop of horse, led by its lieutenant—Rawley or Rowley, who was a Leveller—and this troop had declared for the *Agreement of the People* earlier in the year. Thompson was said to be 'the man who draws all men after him' and his following grew to between 300 and 400.[27] His intention was to raise a regiment of horse. It was said that he appointed officers and NCOs and gave out commissions to raise men:

> Whereas I WT am a freeborn commoner of England, I am resolved to raise a regiment of horse for the defence of the liberties and freedom of my fellow commoners; and therefore do hereby authorise and appoint you HL to raise a troop of horse, and them to lead, etc, obeying such orders and directions, which from time to time you shall receive from me, or other your superior officer.

'In which, it's observable', was a pointed comment, 'that by the very same principles he grounds this commission on, he usurps power himself over others, who upon the same foundation, have as much right thereunto, as himself'.[28]

The relationship between Thompson's action and the mutiny at Salisbury is unclear. One of the leading Salisbury mutineers was John Wood, who had been Thompson's fellow prisoner at Windsor after the mutiny at Corkbush Field in 1647; and another was Cornet James Thompson, who was repeatedly identified in the press as his brother, and subsequently executed at Burford for mutiny. It is clear that Thompson

26 A Woolrych, op cit, p344; A L Morton (ed), *Freedom in Arms* (London, 1975), p68; H N Brailsford, op cit, p513; Taft's entry for William Thompson in R Greaves and R Zaller (eds), op cit.

27 *The Moderate* (2-9 January 1649); *The Impartiall Intelligencer* (2-9 May 1649); *A Modest Narrative of Intelligence* (5-12 May 1649); *Perfect Occurrences* (4-11 May 1649); *The Kingdomes Weekly Intelligencer* (8-15 May 1649); *The Levellers Remonstrance* (1649); *The Declaration of Lieutenant-General Crumwel Concerning the Levellers* (London, 1649).

28 *The Kingdomes Faithfull and Impartiall Scout* (18-25 May 1649).

banked on a widespread revolt in the army. The timing of his action may have been decided by knowing of the mutiny in Scroope's regiment, and he expected mutinies also in the regiments of Skippon and Harrison, no doubt because he and the Levellers had been in contact with radical soldiers in those regiments. His manifesto declared support for 'the late proceedings in Colonel Scroope's, Colonel Harrison's, and Major-General Skippon's regiments...resolving to live and die with them, in their and our just and mutual defence'. He may have intended to join with them, but Skippon's regiment remained quiescent and only two troops of Harrison's regiment mutinied. Thompson's rising was doomed because the great bulk of the army did not revolt.

Thompson went with 120 horse to Coventry on 9 May but the gates were shut against him and he withdrew without attempting to force an entry. At Towcester he took the postmaster prisoner and gave him parole to go to London to seek from the Council of State the release of Thompson's three comrades held in Northampton jail. The deal was that if the postmaster succeeded he would go free, but if he failed he would return to the rebels and render himself their prisoner again. A newspaper was shocked by Thompson assuming the power to grant parole: 'Behold how this new general took upon him, all will be generals if this way go on.' Thompson, who believed in the codes of honour espoused by officers and gentlemen, did not realise that they did not apply when against the interests of their class. The Council of State did not release the three prisoners at Northampton and the House of Commons ordered that the postmaster 'be required not to render himself unto William Thompson, and such others as are now in arms against the parliament, notwithstanding any parole'. Thompson and his adherents were proclaimed 'traitors and rebels to the commonwealth'.[29]

Thompson was not able to mobilise any substantial popular support. It was said that few had any appetite to risk their lives in his cause and that thousands declared against it.[30] People feared a renewal of civil war, with all the disruption and destruction that entailed, and they craved peace and settled government. Thompson's main support came from soldiers, who were highly unpopular because the continuing existence of

29   *The Declaration of Lieutenant-General Crumwel Concerning the Levellers; A Modest Narrative of Intelligence* (5-12 May 1649); *The Kingdomes Weekly Intelligencer* (8-15 May 1649); *The Moderate Intelligencer* (10-17 May 1649); *Commons Journals*, vol VI (1648-51), p207.

30   *The Declaration of Lieutenant-General Crumwel Concerning the Levellers; The Levellers Remonstrance* (1649); *The Declaration of the Prince of Wales* (London, 1649); *England's Moderate Messenger* (7-14 May 1649); *The Kingdomes Weekly Intelligencer* (8-15 May 1649).

a large army was the cause of heavy taxation, and yet the soldiers were unpaid and lived off the people at free-quarter, which was especially grievous in 1649 because it was a time of dearth and depression. Most prominent amongst Thompson's supporters were troopers from Reynolds' regiment and they were hated by the local country people upon whom they had been billeted for some time without paying for their board and lodging.

At about the same time as Thompson raised the flag of resistance at Banbury, not very far away the Levellers of the Chilterns met at Aylesbury in Buckinghamshire. Like Thompson they condemned the imprisonment of the Leveller leaders, but unlike Thompson they denounced the oppressions of lords of manors, copyhold tenure, and payments on entry into a tenancy and on the death of a tenant. They declared their support for the Diggers, who had established a communistic community at St George's Hill in Surrey and would soon set up another at Iver in Buckinghamshire.[31] William Everard was at the beginning a leader of the Diggers but soon disappeared from the scene and he may have joined Thompson at Banbury. A William Everard was a fellow prisoner with Thompson at Windsor after the mutiny at Corkbush Field and he may have been the same man as the Digger, but the evidence is very frail, and it was a different Everard who was with the mutineers at Burford. But the fact that the digging on St George's Hill and the army mutinies were contemporaneous allowed Cromwell to smear the mutineers with the allegation that they aimed 'to have proportioned all men's estates by way of community', and by implication to associate the Diggers with the mutinies.[32] Thompson, however, made no specific appeal to poor peasants or to landless labourers, or to the peasantry in general, and the absence of support from the country people was a further reason why his revolt could not succeed. A L Morton was correct in observing that 'the Council of State, dominated by the grandees [ie chief officers of the army], was firmly in control and could only have been dislodged by a new revolution, the conditions for which did not exist'.[33]

Three troops of Colonel Reynolds' regiment remained obedient to him, who even now may have retained his reputation as a radical, and he sent them against Thompson's forces at Banbury on 9 May, thus

31   G H Sabine (ed), op cit, pp643-647; *The Kingdomes Faithfull and Impartiall* Scout (4-11 May 1649); K Thomas, 'Another Digger Broadside', *Past and Present* 42 (1969), pp57-68.
32   *The Declaration of Lieutenant-Generall Crumwel Concerning the Levellers; The Declaration of the Prince of Wales; Perfect Occurrences* (25 May-1 June 1649); G H Sabine (ed), op cit, pp103-104 n1; B Denton, op cit, p17; C Hill, *The World Turned Upside Down*, op cit, pp228-230; I Gentles, op cit, p349.
33   A L Morton (ed), op cit, p60.

blocking any move they may have intended to link up with the mutineers at Salisbury. On the outskirts of the town his advance party encountered Thompson and his men. Thompson called out for a parley and 'desired to know a reason of their approach, and what it was they desired'. Reynolds' officers replied that they had no authority to treat but forbore from attacking until they heard from their colonel. Reynolds demanded that the mutinous troops surrender their colours and their leader. 'Thompson,' as Brailsford said, 'obedient to the democratic tradition of the Levellers, then called a council.'

> Some moved that Captain Thompson and the colours might be delivered up, but his quartermaster said no, and that they were all equally engaged and that as they had joined together, so they would all live and die together.

This was probably Miles Sindercombe who later would make several attempts to assassinate Cromwell. But Thompson's men were already deserting him: 'divers…went some one way, and some another, some with their horses, and some without', no doubt reluctant to draw their swords against comrades from their own regiment, although that could have worked both ways, and an unwillingness to use force may be detected on both sides. Those who remained would not betray Thompson into the hands of his enemies but advised him to escape while he could, which he did in company with his 'lieutenant' and some 20 others. The rest, numbering about 100, surrendered their colours and submitted to Reynolds, who discharged them, apart from two 'ringleaders'—'Captain Thompson's corporal and another'. Some 60 retired to their homes and about 40 rejoined the regiment—not a great vote of confidence in the colonel. When Reynolds was informed that Thompson was escaping, he sent a party of horse after him. But Thompson, as one newspaper reported, 'behaved himself very resolutely', or as another commented, 'being more valiant than wise', wheeled about and shot Lieutenant Parry dead, wounded another and dismounted a third of his pursuers, and made good his escape.

The weakness of Thompson's position was that he had not had time to concentrate his forces, for Lieutenant Rawley and the Oxfordshire horse were still on their way to Banbury, unaware of the presence of Reynolds and of the surrender of most of Thompson's men. As they approached, Reynolds sent out a party to meet them, which demanded to know where they were going: 'They answered to their friends, it was asked who they meant, it was answered, Captain Thompson.' On hearing this Reynolds' men charged but were repulsed, some of them being wounded and others taken captive. The colonel sent out reinforcements who dispersed the Oxfordshire Horse and rescued the prisoners. At some point before this engagement Thompson had joined up with the Oxfordshire men, but now he and Rawley, with 12 to 18 companions, fled, it was said towards Rockingham Forest in Northamptonshire.[34]

Many of the landless poor had migrated to this as to other forests and settled on the commons and wastes, scratching a living by pasturing a few animals, taking wood, poaching and pilfering. Everitt and Hill believe that such forests were centres of religious and political radicalism.[35]

Thompson and Rawley with a small band of about a dozen horsemen entered Northampton late at night on 16 May. As a result of dearth and depression in the years 1647-49 many labouring men in Northampton were unemployed and suffering from high food prices. In order to prevent the 'many inconveniences and outrages to the disturbance of the peace' that might ensue, the governing body of the town had initiated in 1647 a programme of public works to relieve them, and this may have blunted the edge of social discontent.[36] Thomas Bell, presbyterian minister of All Hallows Church, Northampton, gave a graphic account of what followed the arrival of Thompson and his little force of revolutionaries. The next morning they went to the gaol and freed their three friends who had been imprisoned for distributing 'seditious papers' (this may have been Thompson's motive for coming to Northampton), whom they would have regarded as 'political prisoners', and following an orderly and law abiding course, they did not release any of the 'common criminals':

> And then rode with his company up and down the town to all the gates, and gave out...that they would deliver the nation from oppression of all sorts, and so went to see the ordnance and ammunition, and took the keys into his own hands, and then went to the market cross and read his

34 The Kingdomes Weekly Intelligencer (8-15 May 1649); Continued Heads of Perfect Passages in Parliament (11-18 May 1649); A Perfect Summary of an Exact Dyarie of Some Passages of Parliament (7-14 May 1649); The Moderate (8-15 May 1649); A Modest Narrative of Intelligence (12-19 May 1649); The Moderate Intelligencer (10-17 May 1649 and 17-24 May 1649); A Perfect Diurnall (7-14 May 1649); Mercurius Elencticus (7-14 May 1649); Perfect Occurrences (11-18 May 1649); Mercurius Brittanicus (15-22 May 1649); H N Brailsford, op cit, p514. For Miles Sindercombe see Dictionary of National Biography.

35 P A J Pettit, The Royal Forests of Northamptonshire: A Study of their Economy 1558-1714, Northamptonshire Record Society, vol XXIII (Gateshead, 1968), pp170-171, 175, 181-182; A Everitt, 'Farm Labourers', in J Thirsk (ed), The Agrarian History of England and Wales, vol IV (1500-1640) (Cambridge, 1967), p463; C Hill, The World Turned Upside Down, op cit, pp35-40.

36 J C Cox (ed), The Records of the Borough of Northampton, vol II (2 vols, Northampton, 1898), p180.

Declaration, and made a speech to those that came about him, that he would free them from excise, free-quarter, taxes, and tithes, and exhorted all men to assist him in so good a work; and then went to the excise office and took all the money he there found, and gave much to the poor people that flocked about him and prayed for him. After that he inquired for drums, and fetched them where he found them, and beat them all about the town, and a sergeant made proclamation that those who would list themselves should be well entertained.

Neither the town's authorities nor its inhabitants offered any resistance. 'All this while nobody stirred'; he 'did what he pleased, nobody offering to resist him.' Amazement was expressed that Thompson 'with 13 men kept that walled town in awe'; 'a town of brave courage' was one sarcastic comment. A townsman expressed consternation that 'our people suffered Corporal Thompson and 12 more to lord it in this place 40 hours', and Rev Bell asked the mayor 'how this impudence of a few men could be so swallowed in this town, that was not wont to carry coals so patiently?' The mayor explained that he had called a meeting of the aldermen but few had attended and those that did were divided in their opinions what to do, because Thompson:

> spoke well, and they believed had a great party, for not only the old malignants [royalists] and rabble of poor people would be for him, but all the sectaries in town and country, because he promises to pull down tithes and ministers; that we had no horse to oppose theirs, and they would quell our foot as soon as any preparation should be made, or arms put into their hands; neither knew we whom to trust, all men were so unsatisfied and taken with his grounds, that it was lawful to repel force with force; and if they should engage and get the worst the town would be destroyed.

This reflected the argument that the government was illegitimate and owed its power to force, and that therefore it was lawful to oppose it by force. Also the mayor's response was characteristic of town rulers during the revolution, in giving priority to avoiding the destruction of their property. The mayor added that Thompson's men were well behaved, being 'neither insolent nor injurious unto any, but very civil, and paid for what they took' (presumably with the excise money, which no doubt they regarded as having been unjustly extorted from the poor).

How much support did Thompson really have in Northampton? The lack of opposition from the inhabitants may have reflected a degree of sympathy, but if so it was not translated into active support. He recruited only 30 or 40 men. According to one account they were 'some few of the inferior sort of the town', but according to most accounts they came from the country: 'poor country men' who 'were drawn in with fair promises, and deluded through specious shows of riches and plenty'. As with giving the excise money to the poor, there is a hint that Thompson had a vision of 'the world turned upside down' and of redistribution of wealth from the rich to the poor. But one townsman did not see much positive support for Thompson in Northampton: 'Certain it is here are few Levellers, and as few of that sort called sectaries.' The mayor's inaction was due largely to the fact that he had heard that Fairfax and Cromwell had utterly defeated the mutineers of Scroope's, Ireton's and Harrison's regiments at Burford, and were now on their march to Northampton. It was probably for this reason that, when the mayor sent to the County Committee for help, it advised him not to meddle but to let things take their course, although they did muster the county troop of horse. The mayor now wrote a letter to Fairfax to let him know the position in the town and, fearing that the Thompsonians would intercept it, one of the aldermen, who was a physician, concealed it in a box of pills and directed it via a friend at Witney in Oxfordshire.[37]

Thompson also heard the news of the rout of the mutineers at Burford, and if he had had hopes of help from that quarter they were now dashed. On 18 May his men marched out of Northampton, 'much afraid' and expecting an attack from the direction of Oxford. They went northwards seven or eight miles towards Walgrave, being 21 foot and nine or ten horse. It is tempting, with Christopher Hill, to think that they were going to Wellingborough, a radical centre where there was much poverty and a Digger community would be established in 1650.[38] But it appears that Thompson was skirting Wellingborough and going in the direction of Rockingham Forest, which had figured regularly as a region where he expected support, and perhaps now seen as a place where they could conceal themselves. Colonel Reynolds was in pursuit and overran Thompson's little camp early in the morning of 19 May. Thompson had a good horse and might have got away but he had promised not to desert his foot. He mounted and charged Butler's men, but was shot and though bleeding from the

37 A Perfect Diurnall (14-21 May 1649 and 21-28 May 1649); The Moderate Intelligencer (17-14 May 1649); Mercurius Pacificus (17-25 May 1649); Perfect Occurrences (18-24 May 1649); A Modest Narrative of Intelligence (19-26 May 1649); The Moderate (15-22 May 1649); A Moderate Intelligence (17-24 May 1649); The Declaration of the Prince of Wales; B Denton, op cit, pp20-24.
38 C Hill, The World Turned Upside Down, op cit, p100; G H Sabine (ed), op cit, pp649-651.

wound 'went off gallantly, and led them thus some three miles'. He took refuge in Sywell Wood and staunched the bleeding by stuffing moss in his wound, but 'being discovered, a party of ten troopers rode up to him, whom he charged, fought, and shot one of them, and upon a second charge shot another, and Thompson being well horsed (though wounded) wheeled about again, and rode up to a bush where he made another charge, and wounded two of them.'

He was himself shot again more than once and was offered quarter but 'told them he scorned it'. A corporal dismounted and taking Colonel Reynolds' own carbine crept in among the bushes and as he heard Thompson galloping up to make yet another charge he saw his target and shot him twice in the back. As he fell from his horse and 'began to stagger' the corporal 'to make sure gave him a good blow with the end of his carbine and felled him, and so died William Thompson'. Then they laid him on a horse and shortly before one o'clock 'brought him to this town of Northampton, it being Saturday the market day, and carried him about the market to show him to the people', recorded the town clerk. There may have been some fear that he did have some sympathisers in the town and in any case the people must be made to see the fate of such rebels. His corpse was treated with respect and 'the next day being the Sabbath they buried him the churchyard of All Saints'. His men, including Lieutenant Rawley, were prisoners, but 'the poor country men…are sent to their homes', while 'some others which were incendiaries in the business and seducers of the people' were kept in custody and 'are like to suffer condign punishment'. Rev Bell reported that 'Mistress Thompson hearing of her husband's death, being great with child and near her time, fell in labour, and both she and her child are dead'.[39]

Thompson and his revolt attracted far more attention than Winstanley and the Diggers, no doubt because the Diggers represented no direct and immediate threat to the government whereas Thompson and the army mutinies did. The London press called him 'the great leading Thompson' and his party 'Thompsonians or Thomasons'. He was nicknamed 'Thompson the Great' and 'Thompson the Desperate', 'the General of the Levellers' and the stirrer up 'of a headless generation'. A royalist newspaper jestingly called him 'the great Achilles,

---

39   A Perfect Diurnall (21-28 May 1649); Perfect Occurrences (18-24 May 1649); The Perfect
     Weekly Account (16-23 May 1649); The Moderate (15-22 May 1649); The Kingdomes
     Weekly Intelligencer (15-22 May 1649); Mercurius Pacificus (17-25 May 1649);
     A Moderate Intelligence (17-24 May 1649); The Moderate Intelligencer (17-24 May 1649);
     A Modest Narrative of Intelligence (19-26 May 1649); B Denton, op cit, pp25-28.

or that Alexander of the Levellers, who wanted nothing but a royal cause, and a better fortune, to have built himself a monument as large as either of those'. His obituaries were touched with admiration for his bravery: 'He had the name of a very stout man', 'a man of undaunted courage, but a person very notorious' and generally vitriolic. 'Thus the principal ringleader of these mutineers fell; and as he loved blood, so he died in the same'; 'As a traitor he died in his blood: thus the wicked shall fall by his own wickedness'; 'his actions…are so notorious, as the memory of him is hateful, and his name rots'; 'and so died like a wicked wretch as he lived, and there is an end of the Levellers' uproar.' But he was not immediately forgotten. Sectaries were branded by their opponents as 'Thompson's party, Levellers', and George Foster in his vision of the millennium in which god would establish equality, making 'the low and poor equal with the rich', added that then the Leveller martyrs Lockyer and Thompson would be avenged.[40]

The judgements of modern historians have not been much more favourable, the most sympathetic being H N Brailsford, who described him as 'a hot tempered man, self confident, aggressive and much too quick to draw his sword', but a 'romantic rebel' who inspired a following; and Barry Denton who says that he 'was far more than a ruffian too quick to draw a sword'. T C Pease spoke of 'the disreputable William Thompson', 'a desperate man of bad habits…who put forth a ringing manifesto worthy of a better man' and 'ended his desperate life by a desperate death'. C H Firth and Godfrey Davies said that he 'died fighting with a courage worthy of a better cause', and G E Aylmer repeats this judgement. These historians overlook the fact that the cause for which Thompson consistently struggled and for which he died, was that of the Levellers and the *Agreement of the People*, a cause for which they express some admiration. Ian Gentles claims an insight into the heart of the man and seizes the opportunity to extend it more generally to revolutionaries:

While he was remarkably successful at attracting Leveller support for his activities, Thompson at bottom was one of those figures who is familiar

40 *A Modest Narrative of Intelligence* (12-19 May 1649 and 19-26 May 1649); *A Moderate Intelligence* (17-24 May 1649); *Mercurius Elencticus* (21-28 May 1649); *The Kingdomes Weekly Intelligencer* (15-22 May 1649); *A Full Narrative of all the Proceedings Betweene His Excellency the Lord Fairfax and the Mutineers* (London, 1649); *The Moderate Intelligencer* (17-24 May 1649); *The Perfect Weekly Account* (16-23 May 1649); *The Kingdomes Faithfull and Impartiall Scout* (18-25 May 1649); *Mercurius Brittanicus* (15-22 May 1649); *The Discoverer*, part ii, p19; *Reliquiae Baxterianae*, op cit, p54; B Denton, op cit, p27; P Gregg, *Free-born John: A Biography of John Lilburne* (London, 1961), p281; C Hill, *The World Turned Upside Down*, op cit, pp98, 179.

in all revolutions: the man of violent or criminal propensities who for a time camouflages his lawlessness beneath the rhetoric of resistance to unjust authority.[41]

The whole story of William Thompson, however, seems to show his sincerity and his significance as representative of an element in the Leveller mentality. John Lilburne and Richard Overton both said they would die for the *Agreement*: 'Resolved by God's assistance I am', declared Lilburne, 'to spend my heart's blood against them [the great officers of the army], if they will not condescend to a just *Agreement* that may be good for the whole nation; that so we may have a new and as equal a Representative as may be'; 'that *Agreement* I will have, or else I'll die at their feet', proclaimed Overton: 'I'll have no accord or peace with them at all till they yielded that'.[42] But it was not Lilburne or Overton who died for the *Agreement*. It was Corporal Thompson.

The mutineers of Scroope's, Ireton's and Harrison's regiments made no mention of the *Agreement of the People* or of the imprisonment of the Leveller leaders in the Tower, which were the two main issues on which the Levellers were campaigning at this time. But Thompson did take his stand overtly and primarily on obtaining the adoption of the *Agreement of the People* and on securing the release of the Leveller leaders. While Thompson's revolt was avowedly an action in the Leveller cause and had a clear political objective, it is much less clear how far historians have been correct in calling the Salisbury mutiny (or, as it is usually known, the 'Burford Mutiny') a Leveller revolt. The Levellers would have expected to benefit from it, as dividing the army and weakening the chief officers, and they would have supported its main aim, which was to revive the General Council of the Army, with representatives of the rank and file as well as of the officers, which had existed in 1647 until suppressed by Fairfax. But Lilburne denied any involvement with the Burford mutineers and criticised them for not declaring for the *Agreement of the People*. Unlike Thompson they were not seeking to make a revolution. Their action was intended to draw attention to their objection to the terms for the Irish service and to enter into negotiations with Fairfax to redress their grievance: they were not opposed to the Irish expedition. They said that they were 'unwilling to shed blood, or to be the original occasion

---

41   H N Brailsford, op cit, pp513-514, 519, 521; B Denton, op cit, p24; T C Pease, op cit, pp230 n2, 280, 282; C H Firth and G Davies, op cit, vol I, pp221-223; G E Aylmer (ed), *The Levellers in the English Revolution* (London, 1975), Introduction, pp44-45; I Gentles, op cit, p317.
42   W Haller and G Davies (eds), op cit, pp211-212; J Frank, op cit, p214.

of a new war', but their resolution was 'to stand on our guard and capitulate [ie treat] with our swords in our hands'. They did try to negotiate with Fairfax.[43] For this Lilburne condemned them: 'When they do draw their swords against their general, etc they shall throw away their scabbards, and rather fight with him than treat with him, without either resolving to give or take quarter.' This was precisely Thompson's spirit and he followed exactly Lilburne's prescription, for as Brailsford noted, 'he inscribed the *Agreement* on his standard; he gave and took no quarter'.[44] Thompson gave a clear call for insurrection, but the Leveller leaders made no such call publicly, and at best the Salisbury mutineers sounded an ambiguous and unclear note. The Levellers in general and their sympathisers must have been confused and uncertain what was intended in May 1649. Thus neither Thompson nor the Salisbury mutineers were able to mobilise the maximum of radical support. The decision of Major John Cobbett and other Levellers in Skippon's regiment not to join, but not to oppose, the mutineers, reflected this confusion and uncertainty.[45]

Throughout 1649, whether by 'moral force' or 'physical force', the overriding objective of the Levellers was to bring about the dissolution of the present unrepresentative 'Rump Parliament', and the election of a more representative parliament on the terms of the new constitution proposed by the *Agreement of the People*. In fact, the Burford Mutiny and Thompson's revolt in May brought the achievement of this objective closer than all the peaceful petitioning and demonstrating that had gone before. On 1 May the House of Commons agreed to consider at an early opportunity the ending of the present parliament. On 11 May it discussed for four hours 'putting a period to this parliament'. On 15 May it resumed this debate for 'many hours' and resolved:

> That, in order to the declaring a certain time for putting a period to the sitting of this parliament, this House is of opinion, that, in the first place, consideration be had of the stating of the succession of future parliaments, and of regulating their elections.

43   *The Resolutions of the Private Souldiery of Col Scroops Regiment of Horse* (1649); *The Unanimous Declaration of Colonel Scroope's, and Commissary Gen Ireton's Regiments* (1649); *A Full Narative of all the Proceedings between his Excellency the Lord Fairfax and the Mutineers* (London, 1649); H Denne, *The Levellers Designe Discovered: or the Anatomie of the Late Unhappie Mutinie* (London, 1649); *The Levellers (Falsly So Called) Vindicated, or the Case of the Twelve Troops* (1649); Major F White, *A True Relation of the Proceedings in the Businesse of Burford* (London, 1649).
44   W Haller and G Davies (eds), op cit, pp448-449; H N Brailsford, op cit, p521.
45   *Perfect Occurrences* (11-18 May 1649); *Mercurius Brittanicus* (15-22 May 1649).

These matters were referred to a powerful committee, which included Ireton and a number of army officers. Both Cromwell and Fairfax thought this a very important move towards overcoming discontent in the army. When Cromwell addressed the muster of regiments in Hyde Park in order to persuade them to march against the mutineers, he stressed 'the great care and pains of the parliament in…their resolution to put a period to this present parliament, and to begin another Representative'. Fairfax appealed to the mutineers to submit because the House of Commons had now given priority to ending the present parliament and to establishing 'a future equal Representative'. But when the news came that Fairfax and Cromwell had crushed the mutinies the urgency went out of the discussions of the dissolution of parliament and new elections. The committee did not report until January 1650, and the 'Rump Parliament' continued until forcibly expelled by Cromwell in 1653. Of course there was a problem about holding elections at the height of revolutionary struggles, for it was, a newspaper observed, a business that 'required great care, and some deliberation; for if this nation be a Free State now, it's a question what they may be hereafter, if a new Representative should be chosen of another judgement'.[46]

The conclusions of Charles, Louise and Richard Tilly, in their study of collective action in Europe from 1830 to 1930, are applicable to earlier periods: 'In the history we have been examining, holders of power never granted rights without pressure': 'in the countries we have been studying no major political rights came into being' without readiness of some portions of the groups claiming those rights to engage in collective violence 'to overcome the resistance of the government and of other groups'. 'For a powerful group, almost by definition, it will rarely make sense to choose a means of collective action which currently has a high probability of producing violence; the main exception is when the violence is likely to cripple a significant opponent.' But for a powerless group it may make more sense, if only to draw attention to their grievance, or to have their claims heard, or when petitioning and demonstrating fail:

> The range of collective actions open to a relatively powerless group is normally very small. Its programme, its forms of actions, its very existence

46 *Commons Journals*, vol VI (1648-51); pp199, 208, 210; B Worden, *The Rump Parliament 1648-1653* (Cambridge, 1974) pp146-147, 188-189, 193-194; *Perfect Occurrences* (4-11 May 1649 and 11-18 May 1649); *A Perfect Diurnall* (7-14 May 1649); *The Kingdomes Weekly Intelligencer* (8-15 May 1649); *A Moderate Intelligence* (17-24 May 1649); *A Declaration From His Excellencie* (London, 1649); *The Perfect Weekly Account* (9-16 May 1649).

are likely to be illegal, hence subject to violent repression. As a consequence, such a group chooses between taking actions which had high probability of bringing on a violent response (but which have some chance of reaching the group's goals) and taking no action at all (thereby assuring the defeat of the group's goals)...

For these various reasons, we should be surprised to discover very many initially powerless groups which accomplished any significant part of their objectives without some involvement in violence.[47]

The question is whether the Levellers could have achieved their programme without armed insurrection. Gerald Aylmer is one of the few historians to have considered this. He judges that the plans of the Levellers were 'in contemporary terms' revolutionary, and he lists male household suffrage in parliamentary elections, restriction of the power of central government, abolition of central lawcourts, and devolving of power to local courts and to elected local officers. Although the political power of the old ruling class was partially in eclipse, it would have been further undermined by such a programme. It would have been resisted by the landed gentry in the counties, the merchant oligarchies in the towns, and the lawyers and the clergy, probably leading, in Aylmer's view to 'large scale violence, bloodshed, and temporary dictatorship'.[48]

As Lukács said:

A class accustomed by tradition going back for many generations to the enjoyment of privileges and the exercise of power will never resign itself merely because of a single defeat [and will view] a temporary shift in the balance of power [as one] which can be reversed tomorrow.[49]

The options open to the Levellers in 1649 were limited. Their hopes of influencing parliament or the army officers by petitions and peaceful demonstrations were evaporating. They were faced with growing repression: the government was seeking to silence their press, their petition at the end of March was declared treasonable, and, at four o'clock in the morning of 28 March, two regiments were deployed to arrest their leaders, who were imprisoned in the Tower of London without charge or trial.[50] The new version of the *Agreement of the*

47 C Tilly, L Tilly and R Tilly, op cit, pp280-285.
48 G E Aylmer, op cit, pp50-52.
49 G Lukács, *History and Class Consciousness*, translated by R Livingstone (London, 1971), p266.
50 *Commons Journals*, vol VI (1648-51), pp174-175; *Calendar of State Papers Domestic 1649-1650*, pp55, 56, 57-58, 59-60, 67, 127; W Haller and G Davies (eds), op cit, pp191-192, 214-219, 234-235, 247-249.

People, which the leaders issued from the Tower on 1 May and became Thompson's standard, demanded 'that this present parliament shall end the first Wednesday in August next 1649, and henceforth be of no power or authority; and in the meantime shall order and direct the election of a new and equal Representative according to the true intent of this our *Agreement*... We agree, if the present parliament shall omit to order such election or meeting of a new Representative', the people of their own accord shall proceed to elect a new parliament, albeit with the existing constituencies and qualifications for the franchise rather than with those projected by the *Agreement*, but excluding royalists from voting and members of the present parliament from being re-elected: 'it being most unreasonable that we should either be kept from new, frequent and successive Representatives, or that the supreme authority should fall into the hands of such as have manifested disaffection to our common freedom, and endeavoured the bondage of the nation'.[51]

The 'Rump' did not respond, and when the deadline passed, the Levellers called for each regiment in the army and each county to choose two representatives to a constitutional convention to consider and adopt the principles of the *Agreement of the People*, and to hold elections to a new parliament in accordance with its provisions. This was a strategy with a high probability of violence in that two assemblies and centres of power would have confronted each other, each claiming to represent 'the people' and be supreme. The struggle between them would have been resolved by whichever secured the allegiance of the army, and most likely the fracturing of loyalties would have led to armed conflict. But the Leveller leaders would have sought some sort of popular mandate before such a confrontation, something which Thompson had failed to do before resorting to arms in May. Of course, such a strategy could not be implemented because the Levellers were too weakened and their popular support too small, but certainly by August and September 1649 Lilburne had come to reject the tactics of petitioning parliament and the generals.[52]

Already in March there had been talk of the Levellers organising a refusal to pay taxes and tithes. Thompson said that the aim of his revolt in May was 'to stop the payment of all taxes or assessments

51   D M Wolfe (ed), op cit, pp403-404.
52   J Lilburne, *An Impeachment of High Treason Against Oliver Cromwel* (London, 1649); *The Levellers (Falsly So Called) Vindicated, or the Case of the Twelve Troops* (1649); *An Outcry of the Youngmen and Apprentices of London* (1649); J Lilburne, *Strength out of Weaknesse* (London, 1649); *The Remonstrance of Many Thousands of the Free-People of England* (London, 1649).

whatsoever, as of excise, tithes, and the tax of ninety thousand pounds *per mensem*, etc'. In September the Levellers' *Remonstrance of Many Thousands of the Free-People of England* declared: 'We utterly deny the payment of all taxes, assessments, tithes'.[53] In the wake of Thompson's insurrection and the army mutinies a letter published in the left wing newspaper, *The Moderate*, questioned:

> ...that those who have been faithful and honest to the free people's quarrel, may not have too much cause given them to procure their ends in such a way, through necessity, which in judgement they would not, if those lawful things they so much desire, and strive for, may be other ways granted or accomplished, for the good of this nation.[54]

In September armed revolt was again attempted, this time based on Colonel Ingoldsby's regiment of foot, which had been raised in Buckinghamshire and was stationed at Oxford. At the time of the Burford Mutiny it had expressed support for 'an *Agreement* made amongst the faithful people of this nation', which would include provision for the certain beginning and ending of future parliaments and for the removing of grievances. Led by a Leveller, Sergeant John Radman, this regiment mutinied in September and issued a manifesto 'directed to all the soldiers of the army and to the whole nation', calling for the implementation of the *Agreement of the People*—'an unparalleled expedient for the settlement of the nation'—the ending of the present parliament and the election of a new one 'by the people in general'.[55] The collapse of this mutiny effectively suppressed the Leveller movement until its brief revival in 1659. Dow says that 'when the party machine did come out in favour of mass armed rebellion' in September 1649 'it was merely the last fling of a dying movement'.[56] But it was not a sharp change of policy or deviation, because the party had been moving in that direction for some time. 'Moral force' and 'physical force' had always coexisted at the heart of the ideology of the movement, and as the situation developed from March onwards physical

---

53   *The Moderate Intelligencer* (8-15 March 1649); *Mercurius Pragmaticus* (13-20 March 1649); W Thompson, *Englands Standard Advanced* (1649); *The Remonstrance of Many Thousands of the Free-People of England*, op cit.
54   *The Moderate* (22-29 May 1649).
55   *A Full Narative of All the Proceedings Between His Excellency the Lord Fairfax and the Mutineers* (London, 1649), p13; *The Representation of Colonell Inglesby's Regiment in the Garrison of Oxford, in the Behalf of Our Selves and all the Nation* (1649); C H Firth, 'The Mutiny of Col Ingoldsby's Regiment at Oxford in September 1649', *Proceedings of the Oxford Archaeological and Historical Society* (1884); C H Firth and G Davies, op cit, vol I, pp372-380.
56   F D Dow, op cit, p50.

force or armed revolt came to be seen as the only defence left against the violence of the government, the only means of removing a regime with no legal or constitutional validity but the right of the sword, and so 'settling the freedoms and liberties of the people upon the permanent and sure foundation of a popular agreement'.[57]

William Thompson and Gerrard Winstanley were both revolutionaries. Thompson sought primarily a political revolution and Winstanley primarily a social revolution, and Thompson pursued his objective by physical force and Winstanley by moral force. However, revolution truly is directed at both social and political transformation and involves continuity between moral and physical force. Thompson and Winstanley were both typical of the revolutionaries of their time in that they thought the publishing of a manifesto and the example of action by a small group would precipitate a mass movement. But neither was backed by any widespread or nationwide organisation for promoting their ideas, attaching supporters and mobilising mass actions, and in the circumstances of the time that was probably impossible. The Levellers did have a programme, a leadership, a press, and the capacity to organise petitions and demonstrations, but largely confined to the London area. Although they recognised physical force as an option they made no preparations for armed revolt.[58] Lack of planning and coordination doomed the actions of May and September, and had these revolts commanded sufficient force to succeed, the Levellers had no clear conception of a revolutionary seizure of power and taking control of the government. Had they been successful it is a matter of speculation what they would have done. Hill thinks they would have established a 'military dictatorship in the interests of democracy', and Aylmer predicts 'a popular-cum-military dictatorship'.[59] But perhaps they would have done what they said they would do and held elections for a new parliament. The crucial question, nevertheless, is how they would have been able to expand the electorate, hold elections, and decentralise power without opening the way for a counter-revolution, and whether in preventing the latter they would have had to maintain a strong central government backed by armed force.

57   F White, *The Copies of Severall Letters Contrary to the Opinions of the Present Powers* (London, 1649); *The Remonstrance of Many Thousands of the Free-People of England*, op cit.
58   G E Aylmer, op cit, p50
59   C Hill, *The World Turned Upside Down*, op cit, pp51-58; G E Aylmer, *The State's Servants: The Civil Service of the English Republic 1649-1660* (London, 1973), pp330-331.

The Cooper's Revolt, 1657

There were two main centres of radicalism in the English Revolution: the army unit—the regiment but more particularly the troop or company—and the sectarian congregation. Thompson's revolt was based on the army unit, but the revolt we are about to examine was based on the sectarian congregation. The latter revolt differed from Thompson's in its millenarian inspiration and more overt social aims:

> Millenarianism may be defined broadly as belief in an imminent kingdom of heaven on earth to be established with supernatural help; its inspiration sprang from the biblical prophecies, especially in Revelation.

The Fifth Monarchists were millenarians and they became prominent in the 1650s. They divided the history of the world into five ages or monarchies. Existing society was the creation of the Antichristian fourth age, which was shortly to be replaced by the fifth age—the monarchy of Jesus Christ. The state and society would be remodelled in accordance with the pattern laid down in the Bible.[60] Louise Fargo Brown maintained that there was a 'moral force' wing and a 'physical force' wing of the Fifth Monarchy movement. The former looked to the prayers of the 'godly people' or 'saints' to change the government and inaugurate the millennium; the latter looked to armed revolt to overthrow the government and establish the rule of the 'saints'.[61] But Bernard Capp holds that the essence of Fifth Monarchist beliefs 'was a declared readiness to destroy by force the kingdoms of the world, to invert the social order, and thereafter to be the rulers of the earth'. They proclaimed their belief in violence in most of their pamphlets. But they needed a clear sign from Christ that the time was come for them to take to arms. 'This meant in practice that the violence of most of the saints was strictly verbal, for the majority never did feel that god had called them to arms.' But Capp does detect a difference between the leaders and the rank and file: the former were ex-army officers and university educated ministers and were more reluctant to rise in armed revolt than the latter who came from lower social classes and had less to lose. On the basis of an analysis of the occupations of 233 identifiable Fifth Monarchists, Capp finds that the movement attracted small producers and retailers, that 'the clothing

---

60   B Capp, *The Fifth Monarchy Men* (London, 1972), pp131-132; B Capp, 'The Fifth Monarchists and Popular Millenarianism', in J F McGregor and B Reay, op cit, pp165, 170.
61   L Fargo Brown, *The Political Activities of the Baptists and Fifth Monarchy Men in England During the Interregnum* (London, 1911), pp103-104.

industry and trade was dominant' (as it was in radicalism generally throughout the revolution), that apprentices and journeymen, servants and labourers were also drawn in, and numerous women.[62]

The leader of the revolt was Thomas Venner, who was born about 1608 and came from Littleham, near Bideford in North Devon. He went to London and became a cooper and member of the Coopers' Company in the 1630s. In 1637 he emigrated to New England, living first at Salem and later at Boston. He returned to England in the autumn of 1651. He obtained a position as master cooper at the Tower of London but was dismissed about 1655 after having been 'observed to be a fellow of a desperate and bloody spirit'. Thus like Thompson he was branded a violent man. He was suspected of a design to blow up the Tower and he was alleged to have spoken of assassinating Cromwell, but the evidence must have been very slight for he was not arrested or charged with anything.[63] He became the leader of a congregation of Fifth Monarchists in London, who had their meeting place in Swan Alley, Coleman Street, which Christopher Hill has called the 'Faubourg St Antoine' of the English Revolution, referring to the prominence of the craftsmen and journeymen of that district of Paris in the popular movements of the French Revolution.[64] The parish of St Stephen's, Coleman Street, was a centre of religious and political radicalism before and during the revolution. It was a stronghold of the revolution, but also the scene of conflict between divergent elements within the revolution, containing strong groupings of presbyterians, congregationalists, and baptists, each seeking to achieve its own conception of the revolution. Socially it was divided between rich overseas merchants, 'middling domestic traders', and poor artisans. Coleman Street was 'a large fair street' but 'the alleys leading off it were filled with poor craftsmen'. It was in those crowded alleys that the Fifth Monarchists plotted and in 1657 Venner conceived his plan for an armed rising.[65] He was not an obscure person, for he had been invited to meetings of senior republican opponents of the Cromwellian Protectorate, which included such as ex-vice-admiral John Lawson

62 B Capp, *Fifth Monarchy Men*, op cit, pp82-89, 131-132, 134-135.

63 *Dictionary of National Biography*; R Greaves and R Zaller (eds), op cit.

64 C Hill, *Economic Problems of the Church* (Oxford, 1956), p255. For the role of 'Faubourg St Antoine' see G Rudé, *The Crowd in the French Revolution* (1959, new edition, Oxford, 1972), p185.

65 V Pearl, *London and the Outbreak of the Puritan Revolution* (Oxford, 1961), pp183-184; T Liu, *Puritan London: A Study of Religion and Society in the City Parishes* (London, 1986), pp39, 82-84; K Lindley, *Popular Politics and Religion in Civil War London* (Aldershot, 1997), p283.

and ex-colonel John Okey, showing that he was not an insignificant person politically and that he represented an important strand of militancy in the Fifth Monarchy movement.[66] His lieutenants were a button seller and a cow keeper, and his followers were apprentices and journeymen, artisans and labourers, as well as women who were assigned an active role in support of the rising.

Venner's plan was opposed by the national leadership of Fifth Monarchism but nevertheless he resolved to go ahead. One such leader was Colonel Nathaniel Rich, a kinsman of the Earl of Warwick, who in the debate on the franchise with the Levellers at Putney in 1647 had said:

> You have five to one in this kingdom that have no permanent interest. Some men [have] ten, some 20 servants, some more, some less. If the master and servant shall be equal electors, then clearly those that have no interest in the kingdom will make it their interest to choose those that have no interest. It may happen that the majority may by law, not in a confusion, destroy property; there may be a law enacted that there shall be an equality of goods and estate.

Capp observes that 'the desperate Fifth Monarchism' of Venner's congregation 'was very different from the creed of Colonel Rich': 'Their millennial dreams were sharpened by poverty and they had no social position at stake to restrain them.' Christopher Hill also calls it a 'revolt of desperation' by 'activist plebeian' Fifth Monarchists, who 'saw Christ's cause foundering in the '50s' and 'were goaded into direct action by a combination of impatience and despair'. They had 'no positive backing from Fifth Monarchist preachers or Fifth Monarchists in the army', but they were persuaded by the backslidings of the army and of the governments of the Commonwealth and the Protectorate in the 1650s that they could rely only on themselves, with 'miraculous divine assistance', to establish Christ's kingdom in England.[67]

Such rebels were up against the prime fact of the 1650s that governments were backed by a substantial standing army, professionally led and well disciplined, which was called in 'to deal with riotous

---

66 S R Gardiner, *History of the Commonwealth and Protectorate 1649-1656*, vol IV (1894-1901, reprinted Adlestrop, Gloucester, 1989), pp259-267; L Fargo Brown, op cit, pp108-111; B Capp, *Cromwell's Navy: The Fleet and the English Revolution* (Oxford, 1989), pp142-147.

67 B Capp, *The Fifth Monarchy Men*, op cit, pp86, 135, and 'The Fifth Monarchists and Popular Millenarianism', op cit, pp171-172; J T Rutt (ed), *Diary of Thomas Burton*, vol II (4 vols, London, 1828), p4; A S P Woodhouse (ed), op cit, pp63-64; C Hill, *Milton and the English Revolution*, op cit, pp283-284, and *The Experience of Defeat* (London, 1984), ch 3.

expressions of dissent by brute force'. Troops were used to put down disturbances over enclosures in the Forest of Dean, the fens of Lincolnshire and Cambridgeshire, and Enfield Chase, and to break the strike of keelmen at Newcastle. Resistance by right or left was inhibited by the military presence. But the strength of Cromwell's army should not be exaggerated. Most of it was occupying Scotland and Ireland. The strength of the army in England was about 13,500 officers and men, and they were widely dispersed over the country, with a relatively light presence in London. A large and widespread revolt would have stretched their resources and might have been difficult to put down.[68] It was to this problem that Venner and his fellow planners of revolt addressed themselves in the first place. It is important to note that this revolt was not a spontaneous and unplanned outburst by 'fanatics' (as their opponents called them): it was a military operation coolly and carefully planned and prepared over at least several weeks, and recorded in a manuscript journal probably compiled by Venner himself.

On 15 March 1657 they sent three of their 'brothers' to view the country within a radius of ten miles east and west of London, 'to [see] what soldiers lay therein, [and] how they were dispersed'. They reported back that there were no troops of horse within 40 miles of the capital, except one troop at Islington with two companies of foot, and another troop at Barnet and Enfield, but there were foot soldiers in every town. The rising was fixed for 7 April and at this stage the plan was to 'fall upon a troop of horse and execute their officers and all others of the guards or private soldiers that shall oppose us, and take their horses to horse our men, because the Lord has need, and to receive to mercy those of the soldiers that shall submit themselves'.[69]

A 'brother' was sent to 'buy a map of England and Wales together, and a map of every particular shire in England by itself at large, for discovering all bridges, woods and highways, and that they also buy some prospective glasses [ie field-glasses]'. Two 'brothers' were sent to spy out again the location of army units, to find a place in woodland for a rendezvous and 'some little house or a room in a house' where they could store their arms, near 'some great market town' where they could proclaim and distribute their manifesto. On 4 April the 'brothers' reported back 'that there is not any troops of horse neither troopers either at

68   J Morrill and J Walter, op cit, p146; A Woolrych, 'The Cromwellian Protectorate: A Military Dictatorship?', *History*, vol 75, no 244 (1990), p214.
69   C Burrage, 'The Fifth Monarchy Insurrections', *English Historical Review*, vol XXV (1910), pp728-731.

Epping Forest or any of those roads, neither elsewhere in their journey as directed, save about 12 troopers at Barnet and the towns thereabout to keep the Chases of Enfield, neither any they could hear of within 30 or 40 miles or London'. Now the rising was fixed for 10 April. It was resolved to hold their rendezvous in Epping Forest and to issue their proclamation at Chelmsford, 'because that is the shire town and a great market'.[70]

Incidentally, the information about the stationing of troops near Enfield Chase is revealing of the current role of the army in maintaining enclosure and putting down popular resistance. When the Cromwellian regime disposed of certain royal forests, it sold part of Enfield Chase in Middlesex to a number of senior army officers. The Chase was open land, some of it wooded, on which the inhabitants of Enfield and Edmonton had ancient rights of common to pasture cattle and to take wood. The officers proceeded to divide up their part of the Chase into separate farms and enclose them, erect houses and outbuildings, plough up the pastures and plant corn. The inhabitants protested that their 'just rights' were 'forced from them by strong hand', and in that part of the Chase left to them they could not maintain anything like their previous numbers of cattle. Subsequently, in 1659, there would be serious rioting against the enclosures and a clash with the soldiers resulting in deaths and injuries:

> Whereas in the enclosure riots of the 1640s...the enemy appeared as the king or parliament or both, now it appeared as the army. Peasant discontent was aggravated by the revolution and not harnessed in support of the revolution.[71]

It is important for understanding a movement such as Venner's, which is labelled 'millenarian', what in practice that meant. In the first place it had an experimental quality in that the intention was to test whether they were correctly interpreting god's will, and in the second place they did not rely merely on divine intervention but also on precipitating a mass movement:

> That the manner of the work may be like the case of Israel in their coming from Egypt, and as the visible preaching of the Gospel (and

70   C Burrage, op cit, pp733-734.
71   D O Pam, *The Rude Multitude: Enfield and the Civil War*, Edmonton Hundred Historical Society, Occasional Paper (new series) 33 (1977), pp10-12; B Sharp, 'Rural Discontent and the English Revolution', in R C Richardson (ed), *Town and Countryside in the English Revolution* (Manchester, 1992), pp267-268; B Manning, *Aristocrats, Plebeians and Revolution in England 1640-1660* (London, 1996), pp125-126.

herein they giving the testimony from this city) to his people, and aheighting [raising on high] our testimony, and for the gathering together into one the Lord's people in the counties that were not risen out of their holes till some such call as this, and then that the work may be carried on by them, [that] we may know the mind and will of god more particularly.

Their Declaration would be published at Chelmsford on 10 April 'to invite all to stand up for Christ and their own liberties, and so to dispose and disperse the Declaration among the country people, who will carry and spread them abroad, so that it will be a seed sown'. Then they would march to Suffolk and Norfolk, 'because there is most churches and Christians of their faith, and the country generally enclosed and so most fit for our purpose'. The latter point illustrates that millenarianism was not incompatible with attention to practical details: in enclosed country it would be easier for the rebels to move undetected by the army, and if detected it would provide them with defensible positions and make it harder for the army to concentrate forces against them. Their plan was to avoid confrontation with the army until they had gained wide support.[72]

They printed large numbers of their Declaration, which must have cost them money, and gave a supply to 'the meeting of sisters' to distribute to the churches in London and generally about the city on 10-11 April. Other copies were sent by carrier and post into the counties. They had managed to accumulate powder, bullets and pistols, and to obtain horses, and they had a further supply of their Declaration to take with them to Epping Forest for distribution at Chelmsford. They planned to gather their followers at three different points in London on the night of 9 April and then to go to a general rendezvous at Mile End, from where at midnight they would ride to Epping Forest.[73]

Their Declaration was a collective statement which was signed by William Medley (Venner's son-in-law) in the capacity of 'scribe'. Zagorin describes it as 'the most important statement of political principles which the millenarians put forward'. It showed that the revolt was directed against Oliver Cromwell who, they said, had 'apostatised from his professions and avowed principles', and had 'left the cause and work the Lord so eminently owned him in'. He was condemned for failing to abolish tithes (compulsory payments for support of the clergy of the established church) and to reform the legal

72   C Burrage, op cit, pp733-734.
73   Ibid, p736; L Fargo Brown, op cit, p117.

system, and for 'oppressing the people by taxing them to maintain a constant standing army to uphold his interest and lordship over them'. They intended to inaugurate the reign of 'King Jesus' in place of 'King Oliver' (it is significant for the timing of the revolt that it occurred when parliament was offering Cromwell the crown and he was debating whether to accept it). They proclaimed that they would execute 'the righteous judgements and vengeance of the Lord...upon the Beast and false prophet, the kings of the earth and their armies, and all the inhabitants and powers of Babylon, by the hands of the saints unto whom god hath given that honour', so that 'all earthly governments and worldly constitutions may be broken' and replaced by the rule of Christ and his saints. 'The supreme absolute legislative power and authority to make laws for the governing of the nations, and the good and well being of mankind, is originally and essentially in the Lord Jesus Christ', whose will is revealed in the Bible, which is to be a constant and standing rule in all things. They expected to reverse many of the consequences of the Fall of Man and original sin which had corrupted man and nature. They would inaugurate the millennium in which humans would shed their 'beastlike and brutish nature and principles', 'from whence has proceeded all murders, thefts, rebellion, violence, oppression, ravening and devouring his fellow creatures', and the earth itself would cease to be defiled with 'thorns, briars, thistles, weeds, etc' and vermin. They sought to overcome the conviction that human nature was sinful and the world a place of sinners, which, as Christopher Hill shows, was one of the biggest obstacles to conceiving the possibility of radical change for the better.[74]

Their Declaration continued that Christ's power would be exercised through a supreme council, which would be elected annually by 'the whole body of the saints'—'the Lord's freemen'. This council would exercise the functions of the executive government, including control of the army and navy. The legal system would be decentralised. There would be a court sitting every three months in each county, dealing with civil cases involving large sums and criminal charges liable to the death penalty, with a right of appeal to the supreme council; and a court sitting once a month in 'every market town of value, for the said towns and villages near to them', dealing with civil cases of less value and criminal charges liable to corporal punishment or a fine, with a right of appeal to the county court. Everyone would plead his or her own

---

74   W Medley, *A Standard Set Up* (1657); C Hill, *The World Turned Upside Down*, op cit, ch 8; P Zagorin, op cit, pp102-103.

cause and lawyers would become redundant, but the state would pay 'sufficient persons' as assistants to the judges to find out the truth in doubtful matters. The degree of decentralisation was limited by the appellate jurisdiction of the supreme council, from which the courts would derive their powers. Tithes would be abolished and ministers would support themselves by labouring with their hands at some secular occupation or be maintained by the voluntary contributions of their congregations, thus detaching the clergy from association with the ruling class and equalising them with the people, while at the same time relieving the farmers and husbandmen of a burden which fell most heavily on them. Laymen who had purchased the right to levy tithes (impropriated tithes) would be compensated, thus partly overcoming the objection to the abolition of tithes that it meant the confiscation of private property.[75] They demanded 'that there be no longer continuance of that wicked and unlawful oppression of excise, neither of customs upon the native inhabitants', and no taxes to be 'levied upon and compelled from the people...but by their common consent', but left unstated how or by whom that consent would be given. The excise was a tax on items of common consumption and therefore fell proportionately more heavily on those with lower incomes than on the rich. Copyhold or customary tenure of lands, fines on entry into a tenancy, payments of heriots on the death of a tenant, 'amercements, perquisites, and profits of courts, customs, services' would 'be abrogated and clean removed', thus affectively abolishing the manorial system. Finally, the supreme council would not have the power to prescribe forms of worship in religion, or to conscript for military or naval service. Conscription fell on the lowest levels of society, particularly on labourers, and had been a popular grievance since the 1620s, generating, in the view of Mark Fissel, class division and class conflict. The Levellers consistently demanded that it be banned and made freedom from conscription an essential liberty to be guaranteed by their proposed constitution. *Tyranipocrit* condemned it as a form of slavery.[76]

This programme of radical reforms shows that Venner's rebels sought to make a broad appeal for support. In the first place they called upon 'the godly' in general, not just the Fifth Monarchists, and those 'of what

75   *The Countrey's Plea Against Tythes* (London, 1647); J Osborne, *An Indictment Against Tythes* (London, 1659).
76   M C Fissel, *The Bishops' Wars: Charles I's Campaign Against Scotland, 1638-40* (Cambridge, 1994), pp217-218, 223-232, 251; D M Wolfe (ed), op cit, pp227, 300, 405; *Tyranicropit*, op cit, pp23-24; C Hill, *Liberty Against the Law* (London, 1996), pp166-168.

form, opinion, or judgement soever' to lay aside 'all particular opinions and matters of difference…to come in and be united with us in this bottom'. They summoned 'all men' to 'stand up for equity, for liberty, for deliverance from yokes and bonds', and even on 'upholders and supporters' of the existing regime in the state, church and army, to come out of Babylon, 'to come from amongst them'. Their appeal was 'that all men might see their interest and concern as involved, as wrapped up, as comprehended in the interest and cause we plead'. Thus they sought to precipitate a mass popular movement, and it is of special note that they sought to rouse the small peasants.[77]

'Apart from their readiness to use violence, their programme differed little from those of other radicals', observes Hill. Zagorin notes that they took over the programme of the Levellers' *Agreement of the People*, except that they would have given power to 'the saints' rather than to 'the people'.[78] That was a crucial difference, for with the Levellers power ascended from 'the people' but with the Fifth Monarchists it descended from the godly elite. Whatever qualifications the Levellers required for the exercise of political rights, they never applied a religious test, and they never restricted the franchise to 'saints'. The Levellers derived legal principles from the common law; the Fifth Monarchists made the Bible the sole model of law. Venner's rebels sprang from the radical milieu of the late 1640s and early 1650s. Their Declaration was a mixture of Levellerism and millenarianism. They quoted the Leveller petition of 11 September 1648 that 'the freedom of the people is directly opposite to the prerogatives of the king', but they also quoted the declaration of the New Model Army on its invasion of Scotland in 1650:

> We have not only proclaimed Jesus Christ, the King of Saints, to be our King by profession, but desire to submit to him upon his own terms, and to admit him to the exercise of his royal authority in our hearts.

They spoke of recovering the rights of the people but also of redeeming the rights of the saints. Their programme of specific reforms was Leveller-like and the people in general would benefit from them as well as the saints. Their redistribution of political power to the saints was undemocratic but less undemocratic than the traditional restriction of political power to hereditary landlords. A ruling class which was self selected on the basis of birth and wealth was more undemocratic

77   W Medley, op cit.
78   C Hill, *The Experience of Defeat*, op cit, pp62-66; P Zagorin, op cit, pp102-103.

than one self selected on the principle of 'godliness' without respect to birth or wealth. The Levellers gave less prominence and emphasis than Venner's rebels to the abolition of copyhold. The latter aimed to achieve power by military conquest and, although they promised to respect private property, they intended to confiscate the possessions of those who opposed them, which they expected to be most of the ruling class, and to put part of those spoils in a common treasury for the 'work of the Lord', and to share the rest equally among themselves. They spoke of 'the wicked, bloody, Antichristian magistracy, ministry, lawyers, etc, that have eaten out the bowels of the poor; whose gain shall be consecrated to the Lord, and their substance to the Lord of the whole earth'. They proclaimed that 'the poor, the needy, the afflicted, the languishing, the thirsty souls, the oppressed...shall be refreshed, revived.' There was, therefore a crude and ill defined element of redistribution of wealth in the minds of Venner and his supporters.[79]

The government said that it only became aware of the proposed rising at 7 o'clock in the evening of 9 April, when it received information that some people were assembled near Bishopsgate Street and 'that they were men of Fifth Monarchy principles'. But Ludlow has it that the government had been kept informed of what was being planned by its spies in Venner's congregation, and it had waited until there was an overt act. A troop of horse was sent out and tracked the rebels to a house in Shoreditch, where Venner and 23 others were found in a room praying for the success of their enterprise. They were booted and spurred and ready to take horse. They had 'a great many arms and provisions for war'; 'a standard in white taffeta with a couchant lion with the motto "Who shall rouse him up",' (a quotation from Genesis: 49.9) and copies of their Declaration, 'wherein they set forth a new government'.[80] How many had committed themselves to join the rising is not certain: 40 and more, perhaps 80, and Ludlow put Venner's followers at about 300. They had taken courage from the belief that thousands would flock to their standard when it was set up. Venner and the leaders, 'being for the most part tradesmen', were imprisoned until shortly before the Restoration in 1660.[81]

It should be noted, however, that two years before, in the only

79 W Medley, op cit; C Burrage, op cit, p731; B Capp, Fifth Monarchy Men, op cit, pp146-147, and 'The Fifth Monarchists and Popular Millenarianism', op cit, p175.
80 'The Clarke Papers', vol II, pp105-106; C H Firth (ed), The Memoirs of Edmund Ludlow, vol II, (2 vols, Oxford, 1894), pp38-39; C Burrage, op cit, pp738-739; L Fargo Brown, op cit, p117.
81 L Fargo Brown, op cit, pp115-117; C Burrage, op cit, pp737-738; C H Firth (ed), The Memoirs of Edmund Ludlow, volII, op cit, pp38-39.

armed revolt of royalists between 1649 and 1659, between 300 and 400 rose under John Penruddock in Wiltshire. Involvement of gentry distinguished it from Venner's revolt: out of 139 imprisoned 43 were gentlemen, but there were also eight yeomen, 19 husbandmen, ten servants, two innkeepers, and most of the remaining 57 were small craftsmen and traders. It has to be borne in mind that popular support for counter-revolution came from some of the same social strata as for revolution. Woolrych says that the rising was quickly and easily crushed because it lacked popular support and failed to arouse the western countryside, the instinct of most people being to preserve the existing government against the threat of renewed civil war.[82] Popular reluctance to support the left was matched by popular reluctance to support the right.

The support for Venner was negligible and his attempt was described by Louise Fargo Brown as the product of 'naive simplicity'. But the aftermath was extraordinary and showed the impact that a small band of determined revolutionaries could make. In the evening of Sunday 6 January 1661 Venner and an armed body from his congregation burst out of Swan alley with the cry, 'King Jesus and the heads upon the gates!' (referring to the heads of the executed regicides and so declaring their solidarity with the act of regicide). This time they had the advantage of surprise. They marched to St Paul's Cathedral and defeated a detachment of the trained bands. As more armed men mobilised against them they retired to Highgate and hid in Ken Wood. The next day soldiers under Monck searched the area and captured 30 of the rebels but missed the main body of about 50 which again broke into the city. There was fierce fighting in Wood Street and Bishopsgate and the rebels drove back the trained bands and a detachment of the king's lifeguards. The city was in a state of panic. Eventually the rebels were overcome, many of them being killed or wounded, and amongst the latter Venner himself. Twenty were taken alive, tried and executed for high treason, Venner being hung, drawn and quartered outside his own church. Pepys recorded in his diary a graphic account of the 'great stir in the city' caused by the rising, with thousands of the trained bands in arms and numerous checkpoints in the streets:

> Waked in the morning about 6 o'clock by people running up and down in Mr Davis's house, talking that the fanatics were up in arms in the

82   A H Woolrych, *Penruddock's Rising 1655*, Historical Association Pamphlet G29, (1955), pp18, 20-21, 23.

city, and so I rise and went forth, where in the street I find everybody in arms at the doors; so I returned (though with no good courage at all, but that I might not seem to be afraid) and got my sword and pistol, which however I have no powder to charge, and went to the door, where I found Sir R Ford, and with him I walked up and down as far as the Exchange... In our way the streets full of trained bands... Seeing the city in this condition, the shops shut and all things in trouble, I went home and sat, it being office day, till noon.

These fanatics that have done all this, viz: routed all the trained bands that they met with—put the king's lifeguard to the run—killed about 20 men—broke through the city gates twice—and all this in daytime, when all the city was in arms—are not in all above 31. Whereas we did believe them...to be at least 500. A thing that never was heard of, that so few men should dare and do so much mischief.[83]

Christopher Hill quotes George Wither as saying that if so small a body of dedicated men could terrorise London, what might not 'the desperation of so many hundred thousands...amount unto?'; what 'if the whole body of god's elect in these nations...should engage all together as one man in his cause?' 'But god's elect had never been united even in the 1650s', comments Hill, 'and now they were hopelessly divided and demoralised'.[84] The aristocracy and the bourgeoisie were safe. But the millenarian vision of the mighty being cast down and the poor being raised up, of the high and the low being made equal, and of peace and plenty for all, persisted amongst the poor.[85]

Venner's revolt conforms to one of the perennial patterns of political violence in the modern world set out by Wolfgang Mommsen. It springs from an ideology which condemns the existing order, accepts a moral duty to destroy it, but is vague about what will replace it, except that it will be very different from what exists (Venner's rebels were expecting more guidance from god on the organisation of government and society in the millennium). It resorts to violence because it has no ways through existing institutions (such as parliament or local government) of promoting its objectives, or because chances of achieving its objectives are blocked by the population's passive submission to the established order, and by the power of the security forces. It hopes to weaken the government and undermine its reputation for impregnability, to mobilise popular support by means of propaganda not of

83 R Greaves and R Zaller (eds), op cit; R Latham (ed), *Pepys's Diary*, vol I (3 vols, London, 1996), pp109-110.
84 C Hill, *The Experience of Defeat*, op cit, p66.
85 E P Thompson, op cit, pp52, 54, 128-130, 880-881.

words but deeds, and so provide a rallying point and hope of success for dissent which has been hitherto unexpressed or ineffective.[86]

86 W J Mommsen, 'Non-Legal Violence and Terrorism in Western Industrial Societies: An Historical Analysis', in W J Mommsen and G Hirschfeld (eds), *Social Protest, Violence and Terror in Nineteenth and Twentieth Century Europe* (London, 1982), pp389-390, 391, 401.

Chapter 4

The ending

The revolution emerged from a bloody civil war, and the victorious parliamentarian army—the revolutionary New Model Army—carried through the trial and execution of the king, the abolition of the monarchy and the House of Lords, and the establishment of a republic, which it defended at home and abroad for ten years. The success and survival of the revolution depended on the army, which became 'the salvation, but also the ruler of the republic'.[1] Deployed successfully to crush challenges from the left and the right, the army became incapable of moving either to the left or the right. But there were social frictions within the army because, as C L R James said, 'an army is a miniature of the society which produces it'.[2]

Marx observed in *Grundrisse* that 'the first form of wage labour was soliders' pay'.[3] The rank and file of the New Model Army formed the largest concentration of wage labourers in the country. Private soldiers in the infantry were paid 8d a day—a common wage for agricultural labourers—but the officers, most of whom came from higher social groups, were very well paid. Of the 37 original generals and colonels in the New Model Army, 30 came from noble or gentry families. By the first year of the Protectorate it is probable that under two thirds of the senior officers were gentry of any degree, and one third were of humbler birth.[4] Laurence Clarkson, writing in the cause of the Levellers in 1647, protested that though the officers were often men

---

1   K Kautsky, *The Materialist Conception of History*, ed J H Kautsky (New Haven, 1988), p487.
2   C L R James, *The Black Jacobins: Toussaint L'Ouverture and the San Domingo Revolution* (1938; reprinted London, 1991), p306.
3   D McLellan (ed), *Marx's Grundrisse* (London, 1973), p69.
4   B Taft, '"The Humble Petition of Several Colonels of the Army": Causes, Character, and Results of Military Opposition to Cromwell's Protectorate', *Huntington Library Quarterly*, vol XLII (1978-79), p25; D Massarella, 'The Politics of the Army and the Quest for Settlement', in I Roots (ed), *'Into Another Mould': Aspects of the Interregnum* (Exeter, 1981), p63.

with estates of £500 to £1,000 a year they were paid £4 to £5 a day: they 'brave it out in scarlet, silk and silver', while the private soldiers do not have enough to provide 'shirts for their backs, or shoes for their feet'. Clarkson exaggerated, a colonel of foot was paid £1 a day and a captain eight shillings, but still the differential was large enough.[5]

The rank and file were only temporarily wage earners—many were recruited from small producers and after military service returned to their farms or craft workshops; but others were 'tinkers, pedlars and vagrants that have no dwelling, and such of whom no account can be given'—the sorts of people who resisted being forced to become wage labourers.[6] The army was separate from the system of production and cannot be equated with capitalist relations, for many of the soldiers were conscripts and not labourers freely selling their labour power, and they were not paid by capitalists but by the state.[7] Nevertheless, the tensions in society between wage labourers and their masters were reproduced in the army, where the proneness of that relationship to generate class consciousness and class conflict was demonstrated. This may have been a major influence on the outcome of the revolution. This is not to say that relations between officers and men were uniformly and continuously bad, far from it: the New Model Army would not have been so effective a fighting machine if that had been so, and officers who looked after their men, who were good at their job and 'affable' (the quality which plebeians valued in their superiors) were liked and respected. But there was another side: the life was hard and they were at the mercy of their officers, whose authority was supported by strict discipline and cruel punishments.

There were manifestos during the English Revolution which purported to speak for the private soldiers and which presented a picture of antagonism between officers and men. They stressed the hardship of the service: 'night by night upon the guard'; long marches and rough lodgings where they slept on bare boards, or sometimes on the ground in the open; poorly shod, clothed and fed, and their wages a 'small pittance' which was no more than would keep them from starving, that is when they could get it, for it was often in arrears. They described it as a 'dog's life' and themselves as 'poor and beggarly'. Then they spoke of tyrannical officers: 'Must we not go and run when they

5   B Reay, 'Laurence Clarkson: An Artisan and the English Revolution', in C Hill, B Reay and W Lamont, *The World of the Muggletonians* (London, 1983), p174; C H Firth, *Cromwell's Army* (1902; reprinted London, 1962), ch VIII.

6   I Gentles, *The New Model Army in England, Ireland and Scotland, 1645-1653* (Oxford, 1992), pp31-40.

7   *Marx's Grundrisse*, op cit, p134.

will have us, and whither they will send us? Must we not lie at their doors day and night like dogs to watch and guard them?' 'Are we not scorned and abused, and kicked like dogs by them, as if we were the very scum of the world in their esteem?' 'I appeal to my fellow soldiers, I mean especially the foot...whether we are not used more like beasts than men, like slaves than Christians?' They contrasted their poverty with the wealth of their officers. They pointed out that the officers gained their honours as a result of the sweat and courage of the private soldiers, the rewards for whose labours went mainly to the officers. 'An officer undergoes little or no hardship at all', but the common soldier 'undergoes great hardship with hard labour night and day':

> It is not unknown to you what perils and danger we have [undergone] under you during the whole war, how we that are the private soldiers are they who fought and conquered the kingdom, and yet our officers they have reaped the honour and profit of all our enterprises and sufferings... They have been recompensed and rewarded and we continue still in our old condition of want and misery, and if we have gotten but a red coat, which is a fool's livery, we have thought ourselves sufficiently rewarded and recompensed.

'The strength, the honour and being of the officer...does consist in the arm of the soldier. Is it not the soldier that endures the heat and burden of the day, and performs that work whereof the officers bear the glory and name? For what is, or what can the officers do without the soldiers?'[8] The officers exploited the labour of the soldiers to gain wealth and power for themselves. The language of the protests echoed the experience of wage labourers in the wider society. Thus there was expressed in microcosm in the New Model Army a class conflict in society at large at the time of the English Revolution.

There was a gulf between officers and soldiers in terms of pay, status and power. This may have been exaggerated by the Levellers but at root it was a fact. When the agitation of the rank and file in 1647 secured the establishment briefly of a General Council of the Army with representatives of the common soldiers as well as the officers, it is likely that most officers were reluctant to have 'any co-partners with them in power', and resented 'the sitting of the private soldiers in council with them': 'a council thus modelled was not suitable to their wonted

---

8 *Pay Provision and Good Accomadation for the Privat Soldiers* (manuscript), British Library E537(8); *A Moderate and Cleer Relation of the Private Souldiers of Colonell Scroops and Col Sanders Regiments* (London, 1648); *The Souldiers Demands* (Bristol, 1649); *A Friendly Letter of Advice to the Souldiers* (1659).

greatness and ambition, it was somewhat of scorn to them that a private soldier (though the representer of a regiment) should sit cheek by jowl with them, and have with an officer an equal vote in that council; this was a thing savoured too much of the people's authority and power.' It is plausible that Ireton did ask the Leveller Major Cobbett 'if he were not deluded in his understanding in joining with the giddy-headed soldiers', and did advise him 'not to run against the interest of himself and the officers'.[9] It is not surprising that the demand by the army mutineers in 1649 for the restoration of such a representative General Council of the Army caused Fairfax, Cromwell and most officers to be alarmed. Class differences in society were re-created in the army, which focused the democratic struggle for popular representation on the army itself.

An Act for the Sale of Crown Lands was passed in July 1649 and the proceeds were to go to pay the arrears of the army. The soldiers were issued with debentures which were redeemable in crown lands. But in desperate need of ready cash the soldiers often sold their debentures to their officers at large discounts. This produced a flood of protests. Soldiers were said to be necessitated to sell their debentures for five, four, three or as little as two shillings in the pound to some of their officers, who thus acquired on the cheap lands confiscated from the crown, though it was more usual for officers to pay seven or eight shillings. 'We are forced to sell them to supply our wants', protested Leveller soldiers, 'to keep us from starving, or forcing us to go to the highway, by reason they will not pay us one penny of our arrears any other way but by papers, that so they may rob us and the rest of the soldiers of the army of seven years' service, to make themselves and their adherents the sole possessors of the late king's lands for little or nothing.' 'And you great officers of the army and parliament', pleaded Winstanley, 'love your common soldiers...and do not force them by long delay of payment to sell their dear bought debentures for a thing of naught.' In any case he held that these royal lands ought not to have been acquired by the officers but ought to have been given to 'the poor commons'. A pamphlet addressed by an army man to 'his loving fellow soldiers' in January 1660 protested:

Did not most of those officers...purchase your debentures (the price of blood) from two shillings to a noble [six shillings and eight pence] in

9   *The Armies Petition: Or a New Engagement of Many in the Army, Who are Yet Faithfull to the People* (1648); D M Wolfe (ed), *Leveller Manifestoes of the Puritan Revolution* (1944; reprinted London, 1967), pp360, 371.

the pound to enrich themselves and perpetuate your slavery? And through their cruelty many of our fellow soldiers, who were wounded in battle and made unserviceable, with wives and children starved in the streets for want of bread, while they lorded over you tyrant like. Now examine yourselves whether when you have demanded your pay, you were not had before courts martial and hanged to all your shames, while they robbed you and the commonwealth of your dues.[10]

For instance, on 18 February 1660 two soldiers were publicly hanged at Charing Cross and four others given from 21 to 40 lashes on their bare backs for a mutiny over pay.[11]

At the time it was thought that the sale of crown lands had created a vested interest in the continuation of the republic, but in fact it caused the alienation of the rank and file from the officers, which, as Gentles maintains, 'finally became a more decisive factor than the preservation of the officers' estates':

The memory of how the officers had stuffed themselves with royal parks and manors, while offering their men a derisory five or ten shillings in the pound for their debentures, together with the repeated failure of successive parliaments to pay the army punctually, at last severed the emotional bonds between the soldiers and the Good Old Cause.

In 1659 the soldiers were owed near £900,000 and when Charles II in the Declaration of Breda (1660) promised to secure full payment of their arrears, they had as soon trust in a restored monarchy as in a disintegrating republic.[12]

In a political army many of the rank and file demonstrated political consciousness in the 1640s: in the 1650s that political consciousness bred disillusion with the revolution. In 1659 *The Sentinels Remonstrance* declared that the soldiers have 'since the beginning of these late unnatural wars...hazarded their blood...for promoting equity and justice.' After they did loyally endure and undergo cheerfully all 'hazardous and hard encounters' they became masters of the field. 'Then was it our expectation to see liberty flourish'. But they had

10 *The Levellers (Falsly So Called) Vindicated, or the Case of the Twelve Troops* (1649); An
    Outcry of the Youngmen and Apprentices of London (1649), p11; G H Sabine (ed), *The
    Works of Gerrard Winstanley* (1941; reprinted New York, 1965), p363; W Schenck, *The
    Concern for Social Justice in the Puritan Revolution* (London, 1948), p75; C H Firth, op cit,
    pp204-206; H J Habakkuk, 'The Parliamentary Army and the Crown Lands', *Welsh
    History Review*, vol 3, no 4 (1967); I Gentles, 'The Sales of Crown Lands During the
    English Revolution', *Economic History Review*, second series, vol XXXVI (1973).
11 W L Sachse (ed), *The Diurnal of Thomas Rugg 1659-1661, Camden Society*, third series,
    vol XCI (1961), p42.
12 I Gentles, 'The Sale of Crown Lands', op cit, pp633-634.

raised 'self seeking men' to power, who have cheated them and the people, and subjected all the nation to new oppressions and tyrannies. 'Thus have we lived to abolish the tyrannies and oppressions of past times, but never expected to have erected and established worse as their successors'.[13] Thus in the crisis of 1659-60 class antagonism between privates and officers, and disillusionment with the results of the revolution amongst the rank and file, and apolitical attitudes in others, meant that when some officers attempted to defend the republic and to resist moves towards the restoration of the monarchy, not many soldiers rallied to them. Most of them probably believed that officers were only interested in power and wealth for themselves. The cause of liberty, they may have felt, had been betrayed again and again by their officers, and the revolution had done nothing for the social strata from which the private soldiers came or to improve the lot of the poor in general. As a consequence the door was opened to the return of the monarchy, the House of Lords, and the Church of England, unopposed by the army.

Critical to the outcome of the revolution was that the struggles of peasants (the majority of the population) against enclosures was disconnected from the revolution. Georg Lukács observed that peasants could pursue their struggles with their oppressors under different flags, sometimes under the flag of revolution and sometimes under the flag of counter-revolution.[14] Many peasants opposed to enclosures rioted against those who held and profited from the enclosed lands whether they were royalists or parliamentarians, and their war was against enclosures and loss of common rights rather than against king or parliament.[15] Other peasants supported parliament in the civil war in expectation that it would help them, but found in the 1650s that the new regimes endorsed enclosures and erosion of common rights. The fens of Sutton in the Isle of Ely had been enclosed without the consent of the poor of the parish, which had been a severe blow to their livelihoods because of the loss of common rights. Some of them prepared a petition to the House of Commons in 1645 for redress of their grievance, but seven of their leaders, who were all parliamentarian soldiers, were committed to the gaol at Ely. In 1649 they appealed to the House of Commons, 'as being the instrument under god, to be

---

13 *The Sentinels Remonstrance* (London, 1659).
14 G Lukács, *History and Class Consciousness*, translated by R Livingstone (London, 1971), pp60-61.
15 B Sharp, *In Contempt of all Authority: Rural Artisans and Riot in the West of England, 1586-1660* (Berkeley, 1980); K Lindley, *Fenland Riots and the English Revolution* (London, 1982).

the deliverer of the poor, out of the hand of his rich neighbour, that was stronger than he.' But, as Keith Lindley comments, if they supported parliament in the expectation that it would be such an instrument, their hopes were soon dashed.[16] In 1656 a radical MP, Luke Robinson, speaking for those whose common rights in the Forest of Dean were threatened, warned:

> We promised Englishmen freedom, equal freedom... Did we not make the people believe that we fought for their liberty. Let us not deceive them of their expectation. Is it not by their hands and successes that our interest remains, that we sit here? Let us not forget it, lest we be laid aside ourselves, upon the same account that former powers were laid aside.[17]

But peasants lacked the political consciousness to rise in a new revolution, and either they relapsed from the parliamentarian cause or they rebounded into royalism. In 1659 riots against enclosures in the Forest of Dean and Enfield Chase led to reports that at one of their meetings 'some people of Dean professed that their hard usage at the hands of parliament would force them to turn cavalier', and of rioters in Enfield Chase 'making great shouts and declaring for Charles Stuart'.[18] In these particular cases this evidence is not very reliable but it is suggestive of what may have been reactions of peasants generally.

Marx and Engels observed that in a bourgeois revolution the opponents of the old order claim to speak for 'the people', but when they win it becomes clear that they represent 'the particular interest of a particular class', and popular opposition develops against them with the aim of 'a more decisive and more radical negation of the previous conditions of society'.[19] In the English Revolution a revolt against capitalism as well as against feudalism was for the first time put on the agenda.[20] The richer of the small producers were developing into a capitalist class and economic developments in the 1650s tended towards a coalescence of the interests of aristocrats and gentry with the interests of the emerging bourgeoisie.[21] The rest of the 'middle sort' remained anchored in the outlook of small

16 K Lindley, op cit, pp40, 142-143.
17 J T Rutt (ed), *Diary of Thomas Burton*, vol I (4 vols, London, 1828), p228.
18 B Sharp, op cit, p254, and 'Rural Discontent and the English Revolution', in R C Richardson (ed), *Town and Countryside in the English Revolution* (Manchester, 1992), p262; D O Pam, 'The Rude Multitude: Enfield and the Civil War', *Edmonton Hundred Historical Society*, Occasional Paper, new series, No 33 (1977), p12.
19 K Marx and F Engels, *The German Ideology* (Moscow, 1976), pp68-69.
20 N Carlin, 'Marxism and the English Civil War', *International Socialism* 10 (1980-81), p123.
21 K Wrightson, *English Society 1580-1680* (London, 1982), pp223, 226; D Hirst, 'Locating the 1650s in England's 17th Century', *History*, vol 81, no 263 (1996), pp377, 379.

producers, hostile to capitalism but alienated from labourers and paupers. The potential alliance of the poorer of the small producers, who feared being reduced to wage earners or were already partly dependent on wages, with those who were wholly wage earners, did not materialise. The emerging proletariat was not sufficiently developed to mount its own political challenge to the bourgeois compromise with the old order, or to launch its own revolution, but sufficiently developed to frighten the bourgeoisie into acceptance of the return to political power of the old ruling class, on the foundation of their absorption into capitalist development and of 'a common interest in keeping in subjection the great working mass of the nation'.[22]

22   K Marx, 'The Bourgeoisie and the Counter-Revolution', in K Marx and F Engels, *Selected Works*, vol I (2 vols Moscow, 1949-50), p64-65; F Engels, *Socialism: Utopian and Scientific* (London, 1993), pp42, 62-63.

Index